Conceived in Liberty

CRITICAL ISSUES IN HISTORY

Series Editor: Donald T. Critchlow

Conceived in Liberty

The Struggle to Define
the New Republic, 1789–1793

Lance Banning

ROWMAN & LITTLEFIELD PUBLISHERS, INC.
Lanham · Boulder · New York · Toronto · Oxford

ROWMAN & LITTLEFIELD PUBLISHERS, INC.

Published in the United States of America
by Rowman & Littlefield Publishers, Inc.
A wholly owned subsidiary of the Rowman & Littlefield Publishing Group, Inc.
4501 Forbes Boulevard, Suite 200, Lanham, Maryland 20706
www.rowmanlittlefield.com

PO Box 317
Oxford
OX2 9RU, UK

British Library Cataloguing in Publication Information Available

Library of Congress Cataloging-in-Publication Data

Banning, Lance, 1942–
    Conceived in liberty : the struggle to define the New Republic, 1789–1793 /
Lance Banning.
        p. cm. — (Critical issues in history)
    Includes bibliographical references and index.
    ISBN 0-7425-0798-X (alk. paper) — ISBN 0-7425-0799-8 (pbk. : alk. paper)
    1. Political parties—United States—History—18th century. 2. United States—
Politics and government—1789-1797. I. Title. II. Series.
    JK2260.B36 2004
    973.4'1—dc22   2003018859

Printed in the United States of America

^{TM}
∞ The paper used in this publication meets the minimum requirements of American
National Standard for Information Sciences—Permanence of Paper for Printed Library
Materials, ANSI/NISO Z39.48-1992.

Contents

Foreword

$\mathcal{W}$riting in defense of ratification of the new Constitution drafted in Philadelphia, Alexander Hamilton declared, "It seems to have been reserved to the people of this country to decide by their conduct and example, the important question, whether societies of men are really capable or not, of establishing good government from reflection and choice, or whether they are forever destined to depend, for their political Constitutions, on accident or force." This question, as Lance Banning eloquently tells us, continued to be debated after ratification, with the interpretations of the Constitution itself shaping the debate.

Ideological polarization and fierce partisanship is not new to Americans. Indeed, as the twentieth century drew to close, ideological divisions appeared to many observers to have sharpened in the American electorate. Yet readers will note pronounced differences between politics in the early Republic and contemporary America: The most notable, as Banning observes, Americans in 1790 were still a revolutionary people who were well aware that their decisions would determine the success of the first great democratic revolution in history. This awareness imparted immense significance to political debate over such fundamental questions as the role and nature of the federal government; its relation to the states; its role in trade, commerce, and finance; and, most important, its function in protecting the liberties of its people that had been won through revolution.

The intensity of the political environment in the early Republic contrasts sharply with American political life two centuries later. These differences are so readily apparent that they need not be belabored other than to note that if voting participation is at all indicative—in that nearly more eligible voters do not vote than do in recent presidential elections—most Americans are not very interested in politics. (Those that are appear increasingly polarized ideologically, however.) Furthermore, surveys show that Americans have lost confidence in their political institutions and representatives even as the United States promotes democracy throughout the rest of the world.

Banning reveals the distinctive character of the battle that raged between the Jeffersonians and the Hamiltonians. In doing so, he fires our imagination and invites us to enter into a profound world of ideological debate and fierce political struggle unique to its time but decisive in its influence on later generations of Americans.

Donald T. Critchlow
General Series Editor

Acknowledgments

$\mathcal{O}$ral versions of these essays were delivered as the Leverhulme lectures at the Universities of Edinburgh, Stirling, and Glasgow in the fall of 2001. I am grateful to the Leverhulme Trust for funding the University of Edinburgh's application for the project, to the University of Kentucky for granting a semester's leave, to all the friends who made a term in Scotland such a joy, though it was not the easiest time to be abroad, but most especially to my hosts in Edinburgh: Frances Dow, Harry Dickinson, Rhodri Jeffreys-Jones, Frank Cogliano, and Anthea Taylor.

Chapter 1 draws freely on two of my earlier essays: "The Jeffersonians: First Principles," in *Democrats and the American Idea: A Bicentennial Appraisal*, ed. Peter B. Kovler (Center for National Policy Press, 1992), 1–27, and "Political Economy and the Creation of the Federal Republic," in *Devising Liberty: Preserving and Creating Freedom in the New American Republic*, vol. 5 of *A History of Modern Freedom*, ed. David Thomas Konig (Stanford University Press, 1995), 11–49. A preliminary draft of chapter 2 was completed for a Liberty Fund conference in Oxford in July 2001. Thanks are due to David Womersley for directing that conference and to the other participants for criticisms of that draft.

Introduction

*W*ithin three years of the inauguration of the Constitution, its greatest champions, accompanied or followed by a host of other revolutionary leaders, found themselves irreparably divided over what that Constitution meant and how to shape the Union it had been created to perfect. Within a decade, the division at the heights of national politics had spread into a full-scale party war, the first, the most ferocious, and perhaps the most instructive in all of American history. Never since have clashing ideologies been quite so central to a party struggle. Never, certainly, has such a giant set of democratic statesmen argued so profoundly over concepts that are at the root of the American political tradition: liberty (both personal and public), the nature of a federal union, sound interpretation of the document on which that union rests, the character of genuine republics, and the policies required to set the federal republic on foundations that would last.

As the Constitution went into effect, Americans were still a revolutionary people. Awesome consequences seemed to hinge on even small decisions, consequences that contemporaries thought could literally determine if the first great democratic revolution would survive, consequences that would certainly decide what sort of nation the United States would be. The members of the first administration and the first new Congress were confronted, most immediately, with the specific problems that had wrecked the old Confederation and permitted national reform. Beyond those problems, though, there lay the shaping of the future, and among the leading framers of the Constitution,

1

not to mention its opponents, there were radically contrasting visions of the sort of future the United States should have. The middle 1780s had witnessed a convergence in support of sweeping constitutional reform by men with incompatible ideas about the ends to which this great reform should be a means. Conflicting understandings of the economic, foreign, and financial policies that might secure the Revolution were deeply rooted in the British thought and practice, which had been the starting points for late colonial opinion, as well as in contrasting lessons drawn from the American experience since independence. Hardly had the Constitution been adopted when these underlying differences erupted in a furious explosion. A fascinating story, it may also hold some lasting lessons for the heirs of the ideas and institutions it bequeathed.

Conflicting ideologies, of course, cannot explain a party war completely. Neither can the views of half a dozen major leaders—titans though they were—be safely taken for the views of parties as a whole. But in the new American republic, the thinking, policies, and writings of a handful of the most important men—"great founders" they are often called—can certainly explain a lot. The quarrel started in this circle. It descended from the top, as both sides sought to mobilize the public. And even as it spread, absorbing many thousand voters and a vast array of different interests, the same few men continued to articulate the thoughts and shape the policies around which thousands rallied. By focusing intently on their views, it should be possible, in no great space, to grasp what was essentially at issue and to glimpse the fundamentals that were never in dispute. Three topics seem sufficient as an introduction to its depth and breadth: 1) the incompatible ideas about administration, national finance, and economic policy that flowed from clashing visions of the future; 2) conflicting understandings of the nature of the federal union and a sound interpretation of its Constitution; and 3) contrasting attitudes about the people's role within a governmental system grounded on the people. It will be useful, too, to concentrate primarily on the first three years of this dispute. The arguments developed then would shape the party conflict of the later 1790s, the course of the American republic through its first quarter century, and even its distant future.

It may—and should—appear amazing that the infant Union held together during this ferocious battle. Huge differences between the several regions of the new United States were tightly interlaced with the conflicting visions of its leaders and reflected in the regional configurations of the struggle, which tended to array the West and South against the North and East, the agricultural against commercial interests. Class antagonisms (if we use the term with care) intruded sharply and increasingly into the struggle. Party conflict, in itself, was almost universally regarded as a vicious evil in republics. Neither side could ever see itself as just a party or conceive the other side as anything except a deadly danger to the Union and the liberty that union was intended to secure.

Both parties, nonetheless, were partly right but mostly wrong about the other. Each was truly, from the other's point of view, a fundamental threat to the sort of nation they desired. But Federalists were never, as the opposition thought, the enemies of a republic; and Republicans were never enemies of union. The new republic was the product of a fundamental conflict, but a conflict in which neither party was the undisputed winner (even though, in time, the Jeffersonian Republicans would sweep their rivals from the field). This conflict did not end in despotism or in blood, as such collisions often have, but in a peaceful passage of the government from one group to the other. And surely this was so in no small part because the views of both colliding parties were legitimate expressions of the highest aspirations of the Revolution, and the leaders on both sides were deeply conscious of the unexampled roles that they were playing. They aspired to lasting greatness, human though they were, and in the end they won it, partly for this reason. They were not less capable of ludicrous interpretations of opponents' motives or of wild exaggerations of the points at hand than any later set of politicians. They were, however, capable of being thoughtful to a depth that has been rarely seen among more ordinary leaders. They are best approached as quite extraordinary men who sought to solve the nation's problems in accord with its ideals, and their collisions, in the end, were limited and guided by the commonalities they shared and by their common consciousness that they were leading people through a founding moment that would influence everything to come. Sometimes they came very close to losing sight entirely of the fundamentals neither challenged, but the contributions of both parties were essential to the sort of nation that emerged, as were forces seldom entering into their battle, especially the conflict over slavery.

It will not do, moreover—although many have been tempted—to conceive of their collision as a clash between the left and right, progressive and reactionary forces, a party of the future and a party of the past. From one perspective, Alexander Hamilton was surely the most innovative and perceptive statesman of the age, and it was Hamilton, at first, to whom the others were responding. By way of his financial policies, his economic plans, his foreign policy, and even his interpretation of the Constitution, Hamilton intended to create a modern nation-state—and he did, in fact, lay some of its foundations. His mind was firmly on the future, and his model was Great Britain, the most advanced economy and most efficient government the world had ever seen. From this perspective, rooted in the long colonial tradition, Hamilton was very much a "modern Whig" admirer of the "fiscal-military" state that had emerged in England since the great financial revolution of the early eighteenth century and that, even after losing some of its American possessions, was still the greatest empire of its time. Hamilton's opponents, from this same perspective, were the heirs of Britain's "Old Whig" critics of these "modern" innovations. Their vision is incomprehensible unless we understand this debt and see that modern government, as "modern" was defined by eighteenth-century people, was just what they rejected.

But that is only half the story—half of it at best. From yet another, not-less-valid point of view, Hamilton was seeking to impose on the United States a European system that America had had the great good fortune to escape. Hamilton's Republican opponents, as they themselves conceived it, were the party of the Revolution and the champions of ordinary people. With its written constitutions and its abolition of hereditary privilege in favor of a system grounded wholly on elections, America, as they conceived it, was a new departure in the history of humanity and mankind's brightest hope. In seeking to defend the special social order and the novel forms of government that had emerged in the United States, the Jeffersonian Republicans could understand themselves correctly not as atavistic longers-after-times-gone-by but as true sons of liberty defined, at once, as popular self-governance and freedom for the individual from government itself. Both parties were at once "republican" and "liberal" in their reception and revisions of the great traditions in Western political philosophy, the relative influences of which have been the subject of a recent scholarly debate. Neither side was democratic by the standards of a later time, and neither would be altogether pleased with what we have become. But what we have become would hardly have been possible at all if they had not been present at the start. It should be worth our while to reconstruct their thinking and their story, for "liberty" has always been contested and conceived in the United States in ways they pioneered.[1]

NOTE

1. These caveats seem useful as we start because there seems to be an irrepressible desire to fill the past too simply with heroes and villains, a party of heroes advocating values we approve today and a party of villains we can righteously condemn. For most of the twentieth century, historians portrayed the Jeffersonian Republicans as undoubtedly the party of the future and the champions of "the people" against "the interests." As the century ended and attention to the "dispossessed" became the focus of much scholarship, this seemed increasingly hard to reconcile with many of the facts. The Jeffersonians were led by slave owners. They insisted on states' rights and rural values. Their concept of the people commonly excluded much of the population. Thus, there seems some inclination in more recent scholarship to switch the hats and find among the Federalists the heroes of antislavery, economic development, national authority, and other more modern values. This seems to me as badly misguided as the earlier mistake. The past was not necessarily preoccupied with the concerns that preoccupy the present, nor did the present flow directly from the conflicts of two centuries before.

· 1 ·

Visions

$\mathcal{T}$he argument began within the highest levels of the infant federal government, nine months after Washington's inauguration, when Alexander Hamilton, the first secretary of the treasury, presented his proposals for managing the national debt. Including the arrears of interest, which had not been paid for years, the state and federal governments owed $80 million, mostly to the citizens who held the bonds and other promises that had financed the Revolution.[1] Provision for this debt was indispensable if the government's ability to borrow was to be restored and the nation's honor vindicated in the eyes of foreign and domestic critics.

Hamilton's Report on Public Credit, submitted to Congress on January 14, 1790, recommended that the new federal government assume responsibility for the remaining obligations of the several states, as well as those of the Confederation Congress, and undertake to pay the whole, including the accumulated interest, to the current holders of their notes. The old certificates of debt would be replaced by new ones paying lower interest. In exchange, the government would pledge specific revenues to steady payment of that interest, and the nation's public credit would be instantly restored. With interest payments guaranteed, the bonds would hold their value on the private money markets, where they could be sold if an investor wished, and payment of the principal could be postponed until it was convenient for the government to act. The annual profits from the postal service, estimated at $100,000, would be put into a sinking fund and used from time to time to purchase the securities on private markets. As bonds were bought and burned, the debt would slowly be retired.[2]

The implications of this plan were grander than were evident on its face, although the secretary said enough to trouble several members of Congress. Dashing, arrogant, and absolutely brilliant—he was barely thirty-five but had ascended like a rocket through the Continental staff and into national politics, where he had played a central role in the adoption of the Constitution—Hamilton has been described as "the premiere state-builder in a generation of state-builders."[3] He faced toward the Atlantic and envisioned an arena of competing empires into which America must enter much like any other state. In time, as he conceived it, the United States could take a brilliant part in this arena, and he meant to earn immortal fame as founder of its greatness. But to have this kind of future, he believed, America must first possess the economic and financial underpinnings for successful competition: institutions similar to those on which the English had been carried to the pinnacle of international prestige. Meanwhile, the United States must conscientiously avoid a confrontation with Great Britain, the single nation (with its naval power) that could gravely threaten the United States in war or (through investments in the new republic's economic growth) assist it most impressively toward greatness. Public credit was the key to national power, and a funding system of this sort, which made it possible to handle an indefinite amount of borrowing and debt, had made it possible for eighteenth-century Britain to compete successfully in four great wars with France, though Britain was less than half the size.[4] Taking British institutions as a model, Hamilton was setting out to build a modern state, a nation able to compete with European empires on the Europeans' terms, a nation able to conduct a war without the confiscations, unmet promises, and constant threats of the disbandment of the army from an inability to supply it that had characterized the War of Independence.[5]

Hamilton's design for national greatness was complete in its essentials when he made this first report, although the scope of this design would only gradually become apparent. With proper management, he saw, the revolutionary debt, which had been such a burden to the old Confederation, could be turned into a positive advantage for the country. Federal funding of state as well as national obligations would accomplish much besides the reestablishment of public credit, although this, of course, was critical enough if taken by itself. A federal assumption of the states' remaining debts would also tie the economic interests of a vital segment of America's elite to the success of national institutions and create a counterbalance to the local loyalties that Hamilton had always seen as potent dangers to the Union. "If all the public creditors receive their dues from one source," his report observed, "their interests will be the same. And having the same interests, they will unite in support of the fiscal arrangements of government."[6] Moreover, even as it bound the monied interests to the central government's success, the funding program would erect a framework for the nation's future role in global competition, transforming the government's obligations into liquid capital—a currency supply—that could be passed quite readily from hand to hand and multiplied by using the certificates of debt to back creation of a national bank. Loans and banknotes could be used, in turn, to foster manufacturing and commerce, concentrating capital where it would be employed to speed the economic changes that would lay the groundwork for the nation's economic independence. Thus, the funding program was intended from the outset to further major economic and political as well as narrowly financial goals.[7]

The trouble with this scheme, which Hamilton unfolded gradually in a succession of reports, was that it aided certain men and certain regions more immediately than others. More than that, it deeply threatened other founders' visions of the sort of nation the United States should be.

Both problems were immediately apparent. In the House of Representatives, the funding program stirred immediate anxieties about corrupting links between the federal government and special-interest factions. In many cases, current holders of the debt had purchased their certificates for fractions of their value, often from disbanding revolutionary soldiers who could not be paid except in promissory notes and who had sold the government's uncertain promises for cash. Since the war, the bonds had gravitated disproportionately into the hands of monied interests in the North and East. To pay them to their present holders at their full face value would entail a major shift of wealth from South to North, from West to East, and from the body of the people who would work and pay their taxes to a few rich men whose fortunes would expand dramatically as a result of federal largesse. In fact, it has been calculated that the funding program raised the market value of the federal debt from about $5 million in 1786 to nearly $42 million in 1791. It multiplied the value of state certificates by similar proportions. In 1789 and 1790, North Carolina and South Carolina securities sold for ten to twenty cents on the dollar, Virginia securities at twenty to thirty cents. Sixty percent of Virginia's certificates and 90 percent of North Carolina's were in the hands of large secondary holders.[8]

On top of this, as several congressmen were quick to see, a federal assumption of the states' remaining debts would (temporarily at least) reward the states that had done least toward paying off their obligations at the expense of those that had done most. And by requiring that the federal government impose internal taxes to finance the added obligations, it would tilt the federal balance markedly toward greater central power (which, of course, is part of what the secretary hoped it would accomplish). All of this, some congressmen objected, was profoundly incompatible with harmony between the nation's sections, with republican morality, and with the relatively modest distances between the rich and poor that seemed essential to a healthy representative regime.[9]

Indeed, to Hamilton's alarm, James Madison, the major architect of constitutional reform and very much the "first man" in the Congress (Hamilton's collaborator in the greatest exegesis of the Constitution and the draftsman of the Bill of Rights), soon took the leadership of this minority of critics.[10] Disgusted by the speculative frenzy sparked by Hamilton's report,[11] revolted by the prospect that the victims of the government's original default would now be victimized again, recoiling from the notion that the country would "erect the monuments of her gratitude, not to those who saved her liberties, but to those who had enriched themselves in her funds," this capable Virginian, who himself was not yet thirty-nine, insisted that the case was so extraordinary that it had to be decided "on the great and fundamental principles of justice."[12] He proposed, as an alternative, to pay the present holders of the debt the highest value that securities had reached on private markets, which would compensate them for their risk, but to return the difference between that highest market value and the full face value of the bonds to the soldiers and other original owners.

Madison was easily defeated on his plan to discriminate between original and secondary holders of the debt, which many legislators saw as such a violent breach of preexisting contracts as to absolutely wreck the nation's credit. The Confederation, after all, had pledged to pay a certain sum, plus interest, to the bearers of its notes, and everyone had acted on that promise. But Madison was not so easily defeated on the issue of a federal assumption of the states' remaining debts. Over this, a bitter battle raged for months, provoking threats of an immediate disruption of the Union, until the secretary of the treasury appealed to Thomas Jefferson, who had returned from France to take up duties as the first secretary of state, to help him end the crisis.[13] With Jefferson's assistance, Madison and Hamilton resolved the impasse in an after-dinner bargain. The Compromise of 1790 modified the details of the assumption, making it less onerous to Virginia and several other states, and traded passage of the legislation for an act providing that the government would move in 1800 to a permanent location on the Potomac River, where Madison believed it would be more responsive to the West and South.[14]

In 1791, however, Hamilton delivered his reports proposing the creation of a national bank and federal encouragement of native manufactures. As his plans unfolded, Jefferson agreed with Madison, his closest friend, that the incorporation of a national bank was not within the powers granted by the Constitution—indeed, that the creation of a national monopoly of this or any other sort amounted to a usurpation of authority that could be likened to the parliamentary encroachments that had ended in the Revolution.[15] Increasingly, they both suspected that the secretary of the treasury was following a course that could result in concentrated central power, domination of the South and West by the commercial and financial East, subversion of the federal government's responsiveness to popular control, oppression of the agricultural majority of people, and, in time, a threat to the survival of democracy itself.

The two Virginians' differences with Hamilton were very deeply rooted both historically and in their current context. Already troubled by the transfer of the nation's wealth from its producers to the nonproductive classes, they perceived that the creation of a national bank would deepen the emerging gap between the rich and poor, permitting those who had already benefited from the funding program to enrich themselves again by using their certificates to purchase bank stock, on which there was a moral certainty of profit and virtually no chance of loss.[16] Federal encouragement of manufacturing and commerce would compound the problem of redistribution of the nation's wealth, while Hamilton's lax attitude toward constitutional constraints would favor further shifts of power from the states to the central government and from the legislature to the federal executive. Both the economic program and the broad construction of the Constitution that was urged in its defense seemed to center power at a level and in governmental branches least responsive to the people while creating in the congressmen and private citizens who were enriched by governmental payments an interest fundamentally at odds with that of the majority of people, whose direct involvement in the nation's daily politics most Federalists seemed obviously to dread. In fact, the more apparent it became that Hamilton was following a British model, the more opponents saw him as another Robert Walpole: as a minister, that is, who was subverting legislative independence and endangering the social fabric by creating a corrupted following of congressmen and monied citizens who lived on the treasury at popular expense. By the fall of 1791, Madison and Jefferson believed that Hamilton intended to "administer" the new republic toward a government and a society that would subvert the revolutionary dream.[17] At this point, they urged the revolutionary poet Philip Freneau to come to Philadelphia to start a paper that would rouse the nation to its danger. In that paper, during 1792, Madison and others built a systematic ideology of opposition and called on the voters to support the "Republican Interest" in the fall congressional elections.[18]

The partisan division of the early 1790s can be analyzed in a variety of ways. Like many of the conflicts in the old Confederation Congress, it pitted the New England states against Virginia and its neighbors, states that benefited from the funding program against those that did not, and commercial areas against the planting regions and the smaller farmers.[19] By 1792, however, both emerging parties were beginning to attract a following in every section of the country, showing that the argument involved a great deal more than simple economic interests. As supporters of a strong new government and advocates of rapid economic growth, the Federalists appealed to merchants, artisans, and market farmers—and beyond those groups to many who believed that ordered liberty was threatened by the radical contagion started by the Revolution.[20] As opponents of a grasping central government, which seemed to shower favors on elitist special interests, the Republicans, by contrast, appealed to former Antifederalists who had insisted that a distant central government would threaten popular control, to southerners who had suspected that the Constitution would result in domination by the North and East, and to the rising democratic sentiments of countless ordinary voters who were often special targets for the Federalists' contempt.[21] The infant parties plainly had their strongest bases in New England and the South. Yet the party battle also ranged consolidationists against the principled proponents of a strict construction of the Constitution, enemies of popular commotions against the champions of popular participation in political affairs, and advocates of governmental guidance of the nation's economic growth against opponents of monopolies and privilege who favored private actions and decisions. The controversy split the leading architects of constitutional reform into a group who had concluded from the lessons of the 1780s that liberty was most endangered by its own excess—a group for whom the Constitution was an instrument for turning back the Revolution—and a group for whom, as for the two Virginians, the Constitution was an instrument for shielding and extending revolutionary gains.[22] The disagreement penetrated to the very essence of colliding visions of America itself.

Alexander Hamilton, like most Americans, believed that proper governments are founded on consent and are created to protect the natural liberties that citizens do not surrender when political societies are formed. But while he clearly planned to make the people prosperous and free, Hamilton's concerns were focused tightly on the state, not on the citizens of whom the public is composed. Although he certainly believed that everyone would benefit in time from rapid economic growth, he emphasized the quick development of manufacturing and commerce, which were critical to the correction of a chronic deficit of payments, and he dismissed as selfish the inevitable complaints about the temporary sectional and class inequities that would result.

Madison and Jefferson, by contrast, were committed to an image of a more responsive government supported by and nurturing a revolutionary social order. Sound republics, they believed, must rest on relatively equal, self-directing, independent citizens whose personal autonomy would make them capable of free political decisions and would guarantee their vigilant, continuing participation in political affairs.

The great coarchitects of Jeffersonian ideals were not the enemies of independent artisans and merchants, but they did oppose monopolies and other programs (such as the national bank or Hamilton's Society for Useful Manufactures) that created classes who depended for their livelihoods on governmental privileges and payments. They resisted plans to force the country prematurely (as they saw it) toward intensive economic change, for that could replicate the European factories and cities that divided workers from employers and confined "the lower orders" to a narrow, straitened, and dependent life that might be incompatible with freedom. The archetypal citizen, for the Virginians, was the independent farmer–owner, who produced necessities of life and who, by being free from personal dependence on a master or employer, would be free as well to vote or fight according to his own, autonomous desires.[23] The thinking on both sides was deeply rooted in the arguments that had preoccupied the British as the eighteenth century unfolded—arguments that played a vital role in the colonial decision that a separation from the mother country and a revolutionary reconstruction of the new United States were unavoidable necessities in order to protect their freedoms; arguments that had been reinserted into national politics some years before, had deepened during the depression of the middle 1780s, and were working now to forge the rapidly emerging parties.

The basic elements of Hamilton's design had been prefigured several years before, when Robert Morris, the Pennsylvania merchant–politician who was then the old Confederation's superintendent of finance, had first proposed a funding system. Much as Hamilton would do in 1790, Morris offered two main arguments for proper funding of the debt in a report of July 29, 1782. In the first place, he observed, this system would ensure that "dead" certificates of debt (that is, of promises too poorly backed to trade on private markets) would rise in value, become "a sufficient circulating medium" for a country that had never had an adequate supply of cash, and provide the capital for more intensive economic development. At the same time, governmental obligations would become a new "cement" of union. Looking to Congress rather than the states for their salaries, pensions, or other claims, the public creditors, the discharged soldiers, and the officers who were appointed to collect new federal taxes would join with merchants doing business with a national bank to "unite the several states more closely together in one general money connection" and "give stability to government" by combining in its support.[24]

Hamilton, at that point one of Morris's most dedicated friends in the Confederation Congress, had been thinking on these lines for years. Since early in the 1780s, his private correspondence and his anonymous newspaper series, "The Continentalist," had repeatedly insisted on the need to create among the nation's leadership a class of influentials tied to the federal government and capable of counterbalancing the influentials currently tied to the states. "The reason of allowing Congress to appoint its own officers of the customs, collectors of taxes, and military officers of every rank is to create in the interior of each state a mass of influence in favor of the federal government . . . interesting such a number of individuals in each state in support of the federal government as will be counterpoised to the ambition of others."[25]

Remembering their histories of England in the decades following the Glorious Revolution of 1689, Hamilton and Morris hoped that the United States could imitate Great Britain's path to national stability and greatness. They thought they could combine important segments of America's elite into a single interest intimately tied by fortune and ambition to the infant federal regime, much as standard histories said that the ministers of William III had once created a "monied interest" loyal to the new succession and capable of counterbalancing the Tory gentry. These American reformers wanted to encourage the emergence in America of a facsimile of those related interests—government officers, the military, commerce, and finance—that ordinarily united in support of British ministries and lent stability to that familiar system: interests that the English had in mind when they referred to the forces supporting the "court."[26]

There was nothing necessarily nefarious, of course, in what they had in mind. Hamilton was thinking less of building a committed group of personal supporters than of strengthening the fragile central government against the states and less of fattening the purses of the "monied interest" than of using their avidity to build a lasting and effective state. But even fainter hints than Hamilton or Morris offered that they hoped to reconstruct the British system of finance (in which the Bank of England and the other chartered corporations purchased vast amounts of government certificates of debt in exchange for their exclusive right to certain sorts of trade) would have been ample to produce the most profound alarm.[27] To its "Modern Whig" defenders in Great Britain, the financial system seemed the very crux of national stability and international prestige.[28] But to its critics, who were far more influential in colonial America, the modern system of administration and finance appeared to be a vast, deliberate addition to the instruments of influence and corruption that were driving England rapidly to ruin.

Eighteenth-century British opposition thinking, "country" or "Old Whig," started from a set of neoclassical assumptions introduced to English thought by James Harrington and other thinkers of the civil wars and interregnum: that power follows property, that great extremes of poverty and wealth are undesirable in a republic, and that only those who live on their own and do not owe their livelihoods to others are the masters of themselves and capable of virtuous participation in a healthy public life.[29] On all these counts, the new financial system and its creatures seemed inherently corrupt. Like government officials holding seats in Parliament, like public pensioners or representatives of rotten boroughs, dealers in the public funds or owners of the stock of chartered corporations were dependent on the treasury for their support. Their economic interests chained them to the will of an executive whose aims were always different from and often hostile to the will and interests of the body of the freemen. In Parliament, these tools of grasping ministers subverted legislative independence. Out of Parliament, the unearned wealth of creatures of the new finance spread habits of dishonesty, subservience, and waste to every corner of the kingdom. And while the placemen and the monied interests fattened on the public spoils, independent farmers, artisans, and tradesmen were demoralized by their example and impoverished by taxes that increased progressively with every increase in the ever-swelling debt, which seemed increasingly to threaten that the structure must eventually collapse.[30]

For Americans, it now seems clear, opposition portraits of the failing and corrupt condition of the mother country offered a compelling explanation of the crisis that impelled them into independence. Indeed, to a remarkable extent, the early revolutionaries tended to define their hopes and character as a distinctive people by contrasting their republican experiments with what the opposition writers said was wrong with eighteenth-century Britain.[31] America *meant* virtue rather than corruption, vigor rather than decay. It meant a pleasing mediocrity of fortunes, citizens who lived on their own resources, freemen who could fight or vote according to their own autonomous desires. It meant, in short, whatever seemed to have been lost with the appearance of the modern system of administration and finance—this and everything that might be gained by abolition of hereditary privilege, by written constitutions, and by governments depending squarely on an equal people. Jefferson was drawing deeply on this old and potent language when he cautioned Washington that Hamilton's program "flowed from principles adverse to liberty and was calculated to undermine and demolish the republic by creating an influence of his department over the members of the legislature . . . to draw all the powers of government into the hands of the general legislature, to establish means for corrupting a sufficient corps in that legislature to . . . preponderate . . . , and to have that corps under the command of the Secretary of the Treasury for the purpose of subverting step by step the principles of the Constitution, which he has so often declared a thing of nothing which must be changed."[32]

And there was yet another level to the quarrel, which would deeply influence foreign-policy disputes until the War of 1812. Early in the Revolution, when the Continental Congress threw American commerce open to the world, the economic vistas opened by the shattering of Britain's navigation system seemed as boundless as the prospects for political reform. Economic liberty would complement and be supported by republican ideals. America's example of free trade would revolutionize the world and bring unparalleled prosperity at home. Few principles acquired such general approval. None was challenged more severely at the peace. British merchants bringing British goods on British credit quickly reestablished their connections in the states. Specie poured from the United States to pay for niceties and luxuries that had been unavailable for years. Excluded, now, from many of their most productive prewar markets, native merchants were unable to correct a huge imbalance of payments, and the country entered into a sharp postwar depression.[33] Without protection from the British, the Mediterranean trade became easy prey for pirates. Finally, in 1784, the Spanish masters of Louisiana prohibited Americans from trading down the Mississippi.

The newly independent states attempted to alleviate these problems. Seven issued paper money. Eight imposed retaliatory duties on British ships or goods.[34] But states attempting separate actions of this sort were often baffled by the inconsistent regulations of their neighbors, paper money fell disastrously in North Carolina and Rhode Island, and American commissioners in Europe made almost no progress in their efforts to negotiate commercial treaties. By the middle of the decade, sentiment was moving overwhelmingly toward granting Congress power over trade, power that might be used to counteract the Europeans' regulations. At least in northern cities, it was also moving unmistakably toward new support for economic changes and commercial policies that early revolutionary thought had generally condemned.

The doctrine of free trade had nicely managed a profound, traditional ambivalence concerning commerce that was well expressed in Adam Smith's *The Wealth of Nations*, published in the very year of independence.[35] On one hand, commerce seemed to nearly all enlightened eighteenth-century thinkers an improving, civilizing force, the single feature that distinguished modern Europe most decisively from its medieval past and made it possible for moderns to surpass the comforts and achievements of the ancients. Carrying the bountiful productions of a modern specialization of labor, commerce softened manners, favored the refinement of the arts, promoted peaceful international relations, and supported larger populations at a higher level of material well-being than had any ancient civilization.[36] On these grounds, a few of its proponents carried their enthusiasm to the point of arguing that even private vices, such as selfishness and greed, promoted the collective good.[37] More commonly, however, as was true of Smith, enlightened thinkers recognized that commerce also had its costs. As nations moved from savagery through agriculture to the most advanced commercialization, the benefits proved dangerously unequal. Idleness and enervating luxury appeared among the rich, and as work was subdivided, independent craftsmen were replaced by laborers whose narrow lives and poverty could render them unfit as citizens or soldiers.[38] Smith's arguments for natural economic growth and unrestricted international exchange were something of a mean between the unrestrained enthusiasm of a Bernard Mandeville and the humanistic condemnations of the costs of economic change. The "natural" policy appeared to be ideal as well for thriving, mostly agricultural societies that wanted the advantages of commerce without its social costs.[39]

Early in the Revolution, the dividing line between a civilized society and a debilitated one seemed relatively clear. Mills and shops and trading ships were not a threat to freedom. In fact, increased domestic manufacturing of more of the necessities of life could lessen the country's dependence on expensive imports and promote republican simplicity and thrift, while growing native commerce would exchange America's extractive surplus for more of the amenities of life. The social fabric and the polity would be endangered only if the population grew so dense as to compel intensive economic change or if the nation forced itself into a premature old age by following the mecantilistic policies of Europe.

But during the depression, lines began to blur. Advocates came forward with a more insistent argument for native manufactures, which could offer new employment for the seamen, fishermen, and dockyard workers who were suffering from the collapse of foreign trade, new markets for the farmers whose commodities could not be shipped abroad, and new fields for investors. A few dispensed entirely with the old ambivalence and offered an unqualified defense of manufacturing and commerce in their highest forms, urging policies that would encourage rapid growth and arguing that even the pursuit of luxuries would further the general good.[40] Pro-developmental forces generally supported federal reform. By no means all reformers, though, supported change for pro-developmental reasons. Madison, for one, became the leading architect of an effective federal system because he hoped a federal power over commerce could forestall the very economic changes that a number of his allies wanted to promote.[41]

To Madison, as to the great majority of revolutionary thinkers, the success of the American experiment in popular self-governance depended on the moral fiber of the people. This, in turn, depended heavily on the conditions of their economic life, which would be prosperous or poor in close relationship to their ability to find sufficient outlets for their products. Most Americans (and almost all Virginians) were farmers; and as long as this was so, they either had to trade their surpluses for foreign goods, stop buying foreign imports (and lapse into an undesirable, subsistence mode of life), or risk their personal and even national independence by going ever deeper into debt. Lacking markets for their products, citizens could be demoralized by idleness, indebtedness, or want; and a demoralized majority could mean no end of trouble for a fragile, new republic.[42] "Most of our political evils," Madison maintained—paper money, moratoriums on taxes, and laws protecting citizens from private suits for debt—"may be traced up to our commercial ones, as most of our moral may to our political."[43] Ideally, he wrote, he favored "perfect freedom" of commerce. But this would not be possible until the nation's trading partners generally concurred. British policy, especially, excluded American merchants from their most profitable markets, and, acting individually, the several states could not compel the British or the other Europeans to relax their mercantile restrictions. A federal power over commerce had thus become essential.[44] Greater federal power was essential, too, to force the Spanish to open the Mississippi River, which was not less vital to the shaping of the future. "Suppose the use of the Mississippi denied to us," he explained to Jefferson, and many who would otherwise move west would turn to manufacturing instead, while those who might move west despite the lack of any vent for products of the soil would have to manufacture for themselves.[45]

Pro-developmental easterners, it should be noted, feared the emigration to the West for just the reasons Madison unfolded in this passage. It depopulated eastern states, retarded the development of manufactures, and depreciated eastern lands. Madison was thoroughly acquainted with their thinking but supported emigration and a federal system that might force the Spanish to open the Mississippi precisely because he dreaded the progression to the "higher" economic stage that others wanted to encourage.[46]

Neither Madison nor Jefferson can be properly called an enemy of commerce—not if "commerce" meant the civilizing, comfort-raising benefits of trade. Both, however, were revolted by the notion that the nation ought to move as rapidly as possible to make itself an urban, manufacturing society that could produce and even export many of the niceties and luxuries of life. The two Virginians knew that most Americans enjoyed a level of material prosperity that was the envy of the most "advanced" economies in Europe, and both were deeply influenced by those countervailing strands in eighteenth-century thought that warned that the transition to a manufacturing or heavily commercialized economy could render a society incapable of freedom. Jefferson, with his supreme ability to dress ideas in highly gifted prose, had put the argument in moving language:

> Those who labor in the earth are the chosen people of God, if ever he had a chosen people, whose breasts he has made his peculiar deposit for substantial and genuine virtue. . . . Generally speaking, the proportion which the aggregate of the other classes of citizens bears in any state to that of its husbandmen is the proportion of its unsound to its healthy parts, and is a good enough barometer whereby to measure its degree of corruption. While we have land to labor then, let us never wish to see our citizens occupied at a workbench or twirling a distaff. Carpenters, masons, smiths are wanted in husbandry; but for the general operations of manufacture, let our workshops remain in Europe. . . . The loss by the transportation of commodities across the Atlantic will be made up in happiness and permanence of government. The mobs of great cities add just so much to the support of pure government as sores do to the strength of the human body. It is the manners and spirit of a people which preserve a republic in vigor.[47]

Early in 1792, shortly after Hamilton presented his Report on Manufactures, Madison published a very similar discussion of the proper population for republics,[48] and from the first day of business of the first new Congress, he argued long and often for retaliatory duties on British ships and goods that might compel Great Britain and eventually the whole of Europe to accept the system of free trade that seemed essential to the mostly agricultural society that underpinned the revolutionary order.[49]

Madison and Jefferson were thoroughly convinced that the United States was capable of forcing Britain to accept free trade, and they would pursue this policy with fierce determination and disastrous consequences after 1800, when their administrations sought to counter French and British impositions with the great embargo and other legislation limiting the country's foreign commerce. Most American exports, as they saw it, were necessities of life: raw materials and food on which the British and their colonies in the Caribbean were vitally dependent. Most American imports, on the other hand, were "niceties" or "luxuries" that the United States could either do without or manufacture (at a shop and household level) on their own. America, accordingly, would suffer little from a closing of the trade with Britain, while British ministers would soon be faced with heavy pressure from their starving colonies and from the manufacturers and merchants who would be deprived of an essential market. Economic independence, as the two Virginians understood it, was to be secured—for both the nation and the citizens of whom the nation was composed—by freeing trade to take its natural channels. The promise of the Revolution would be kept by opening the oceanic markets and the western lands that would preserve the mostly agricultural economy of the United States and with it the personal autonomy and relatively equal distribution of the nation's wealth that characterized a population overwhelmingly composed of independent farmers.[50]

Hamilton's ideas were altogether different. Influenced more by David Hume and James Steuart than by Adam Smith or eighteenth-century opposition thinkers, he believed that a developed state would win an economic confrontation with a less developed rival.[51] More than that, although he was as thoroughly emancipated from the old concerns about the civic virtue of the people as was any statesman of this age, he was himself a champion of private liberties and economic freedom, insisting that a more complex economy would not just make the people prosperous and happy but would also furnish "greater scope for the diversity of talents and dispositions."[52] For Hamilton, as surely as for his opponents, the long-term goal was economic independence, but Hamilton defined such independence in a different way. He pictured a mature and largely self-sufficient economic system in which manufacturing would build a large domestic market for the farmers and the specialized activities of different economic regions would combine into a healthy whole.[53] To reach this goal, however, it was necessary in the short term to protect the revenues that underpinned the funding system and would be an early casualty of a commercial confrontation that the United States was sure to lose.

Most of the American elite and most of those who lived by manufacturing or commerce had supported the adoption of the Constitution. Others had opposed it out of fear of the elite or out of a suspicion that a stronger central government would favor the commercial interests over the agrarian majority of people. After 1789, the apprehensions of the latter group seemed rapidly confirmed. It should not be surprising, then, that by the end of 1792 a large majority of former Antifederalists was moving to support the Jeffersonian opposition. But many of the manufacturers and merchants who had hoped to benefit from the adoption of the Constitution benefited only indirectly, if at all, from Hamilton's financial and commercial programs. In practice, Hamilton did very little to support the master craftsmen, journeymen, and workers who were actively involved in making manufactured goods and who had clamored for protection from the flood of British imports. The funding system, in his thinking, was the indispensable foundation for political stability and economic growth. In order to maintain it, he consistently opposed protective legislation likely to disrupt the flow of (mostly British) imports. Tariff and tonnage duties generated 90 percent of the federal revenues that paid the interest on the debt. Accordingly, the plan for manufactures advocated bounties rather than protective tariffs and was concerned more with the encouragement of large-scale manufacturing for export than with aiding handicraft production in the states, while Hamilton's Society for the Encouragement of Useful Manufactures was an unsuccessful scheme for mobilizing large investors in a company that smaller manufacturers regarded as a threat. By the middle of the decade, hundreds of mechanics, artisans, and small, aspiring tradesmen were fleeing from his party for an opposition that encouraged popular involvement in the nation's politics and condemned monopolistic corporations.[54]

In addition, by the middle of the decade, many merchants were enlisting in the opposition coalition. When France and Britain went to war, both of them attempted to deny their enemy the benefits of neutral trade, though Britain, with its naval power, was the greater problem for the new United States. Near the end of 1793, a secret British order of November 6 resulted in the sudden seizure of 250 U.S. vessels trading with the French West Indies. The Federalists responded by again defeating Madison's commercial propositions and securing a negotiated resolution of the crisis. But the treaty with the British, ratified in 1795, acquiesced in British definitions of the rights of neutrals and provoked a naval war with France. Despite these troubles, commerce burgeoned, most dramatically so with areas outside the British Empire, where, of course, the traders suffered most from British seizures and the quasi-war with France. By 1800, many of these traders were profoundly discontent with foreign policies that left them most at risk and seemed to render the United States commercially subservient to Britain. Merchants such as Samuel Smith of Baltimore, the Crownin-shields of Salem, James Nicholson of New York City, and John Swanwick and Stephen Girard of Philadelphia—all of whom engaged primarily in trade with Britain's foes—were staunch Republicans before the decade's end.[55]

Economic and financial policies were not the leading reason for the Federalists' defeat in 1800. For large proportions of the population—market farmers, shippers, and the hosts of laborers and craftsmen who were busy building ships, transporting goods, or packaging and finishing materials for export—the war in Europe was an economic windfall; and Hamilton may well have been correct that this prosperity would have collapsed abruptly in a confrontation with the British. After 1807, when the Jeffersonians initiated economic warfare with the Europeans, this is just what happened. Still, in 1789, the Federalists had managed to appeal to an enormous range of economic interests. By 1800, much of this support had dropped away. And, naturally, as northern artisans and merchants joined with husbandmen and planters, the Republicans became a different party, too.

The change within the Jeffersonians was a beginning, not an end. Until the War of 1812, the policies of Jefferson's and Madison's administrations were consistent with the thinking of the early 1790s. Both presidents were dedicated to reducing the public debt, severing the corrupting links between the federal government and monied interests, restoring the constitutional division of responsibilities between the federal government and the states, and pushing for the open trade and western growth that might perpetuate an agrarian and republican balance of property. The two presidents from Virginia did not dismiss their old suspicions of intensive economic change or heartily endorse the unrestrained pursuit of individual self-interest. But Jefferson and Madison had always thought that individual pursuits of private economic goods would harmonize most fully in a system free from governmental privileges for some or from "unnatural" incentives for the sorts of enterprise least suitable for a republic, while northern artisans and merchants may always have embraced the two Virginians' enmity toward privilege without participating in their doubts about intensive economic change. After 1808, as economic warfare favored the development of native manufactures, the party shifted even farther toward a pro-developmental stance.[56] Party leaders shifted with it.

Undoubtedly, there is some danger of exaggerating this transition. Jefferson and Madison had never stood at the agrarian extreme of opposition to Hamilton's system, and neither ever moved wholeheartedly into the pro-developmental wing of Republican opinion. In the early 1790s, many in the party had objected to the building of a navy, which they believed was needed mostly to protect the carrying trade between the West Indian islands and Europe. Jefferson and others long remained ambivalent about a commerce unrelated to the nation's "natural" needs and capable of dragging it into the European conflict. As late as 1816, Jefferson observed that

> the exercise, by our own citizens, of so much commerce as may suffice to exchange our superfluities for our wants may be advantageous for the whole. But it does not follow that . . . it is in the interest of the whole to become a mere city of London to carry on the business of one half of the world at the expense of eternal war with the other half. . . . Our commercial dashers . . . have already cost us . . . more than their persons and all their commerce were worth.[57]

Nevertheless, both Jefferson and Madison committed their administrations to protection of this commerce, and both expressed an understanding of its role in the reduction of the chronic deficit of payments. And when economic warfare failed—partly, Madison believed, because the British found in Canada and South America alternative suppliers of the necessary raw materials and food—both he and Jefferson conceded the necessity of an expanded role for native manufactures.[58]

The War of 1812 taught further lessons. Armies and supplies moved poorly on the roads and rivers of the West. Without a national bank (since the Republicans had refused to renew its charter), the federal government was a financial cripple. When peace was finally restored, the fragile manufactories that had developed during years of economic conflict were again endangered by British competition. Thus, in 1816, Madison recommended and a Republican Congress overwhelming approved the first protective tariff, a second national bank, and an ambitious plan for internal improvements.[59] Silently, the Jeffersonians admitted that America could not compel the Europeans to accept the sort of world in which the new republic could escape intensive economic change.

Even this did not amount to a complete surrender of the party's old ideas. Republicans could still believe that education, faithful leadership, and an enormous reservoir of western lands would limit or postpone the civic evils most of them still feared. Even the Republican enthusiasts for manufacturing and economic change had no intention of committing the United States to mercantilist economics, Hamiltonian finance, or other adjuncts of the European state.[60] Yet the choice did seem to lie between increasing self-sufficiency and national dependence on external markets that could not be guaranteed. Under proper leaders, the Republicans could hope, a national bank and moderate encouragement of native manufactures need not have the threatening effects that "monocrats" had once encouraged. Land had never seemed to Madison or Jefferson the only source of personal autonomy or virtue. Independent artisans and merchants had repeatedly displayed their fierce attachment to the nation's freedom. Urban members of the genuine "producing" classes could unite with farmers in their disapproval of the idle, arrogant, but nonproducing "aristocrats" and drones. Therefore, as the Federalists collapsed, the Jeffersonians appropriated part, but only part, of their design, synthesizing elements from both of the competing visions that had shaped the nation's struggles. It was a fleeting moment of agreement, quickly challenged by the Panic of 1819, which would revitalize the old debates and set them near the center of a second party conflict. But in that, which is a different story, Democrats and Whigs would argue mostly over means. The fundamental ends—independence and the founding of a federal republic—now appeared secure.

NOTES

1. The debt to foreign governments and bankers, about which there was no dispute, was roughly $12 million. This was refinanced with new and cheaper loans, secured by a pledge of other specific revenues.

2. The Report on Public Credit is in *The Papers of Alexander Hamilton* (hereafter *PAH*), ed. Harold C. Syrett et al., 26 vols. (New York: Columbia University Press, 1961–1979), 6:69–107. The clearest explanations of its intricacies are in E. James Ferguson, *The Power of the Purse: A History of American Public Finance, 1776–1790* (Chapel Hill: University of North Carolina

Press, 1961), 292–96; Forrest McDonald, *Alexander Hamilton: A Biography* (New York: Norton, 1979), chap. 8; and Donald F. Swanson, *The Origins of Hamilton's Fiscal Policies* (Gainesville: University Press of Florida, 1963). The sinking fund, which Hamilton used primarily to keep the notes near par, was ultimately financed from sales of western lands.

3. Isaac Kramnick, ed., *The Federalist Papers* (Harmondsworth, U.K.: Penguin, 1987), 67. See, more fully, pp. 67–75. It has also been said of Hamilton, quite aptly, that he was certain he knew how to do almost anything better than anyone else—and usually could. See Stanley Elkins and Eric McKitrick, *The Age of Federalism: The Early American Republic, 1788–1800* (New York: Oxford University Press, 1993), 95.

4. P. G. M. Dickson, *The Financial Revolution in England: A Study in the Development of Public Credit, 1688–1756* (New York: Macmillan, 1967), and John Brewer, *The Sinews of Power: War, Money, and the English State, 1688–1782* (New York: Knopf, 1989).

5. For Hamilton's life and vision see especially John C. Miller, *Alexander Hamilton: Portrait in Paradox* (New York: Harper, 1959); McDonald, *Alexander Hamilton*; Gerald Stourzh, *Alexander Hamilton and the Idea of Republican Government* (Stanford, Calif.: Stanford University Press, 1970); and Karl-Friedrich Walling, *Republican Empire: Alexander Hamilton on War and Free Government* (Lawrence: University Press of Kansas, 1999).

6. *PAH*, 6:80–81. Punctuation, capitalization, and spelling are modernized throughout the book.

7. In addition to the sources cited in notes 1 and 4, see Drew R. McCoy, *The Elusive Republic: Political Economy in Jeffersonian America* (Chapel Hill: University of North Carolina Press, 1980), 146–52, and Lance Banning, "Political Economy and the Creation of the Federal Republic," in *Devising Liberty: Preserving and Creating Freedom in the New American Republic*, ed. David T. Konig, vol. 5 of *The Making of Modern Freedom* (Stanford, Calif.: Stanford University Press, 1995), 11–49. I have drawn freely on the latter for parts of this chapter.

8. Ferguson, *The Power of the Purse*, 329–30. See also Whitney K. Bates, "Northern Speculators and Southern State Debts, 1790," *William and Mary Quarterly*, 3rd ser., 19 (1962): 32–34, 39.

9. The congressional debate on funding (February 1790) may be followed in *Annals of Congress*, 1:1180–1224, 1234–39, 1248–1322; 2:1324–54. Hamilton, who thought it wise in any case to stake a federal claim to internal taxation before that field of revenue became a state preserve, successfully suggested that assumption be financed by an excise on distilled spirits and other luxuries. By 1794, the whiskey tax was generating popular rebellion in the West.

10. Irving Brant, *James Madison*, 6 vols. (Indianapolis: Bobbs-Merrill, 1941–1961); Ralph Ketcham, *James Madison: A Biography* (New York: Macmillan, 1971); Jack N. Rakove, *James Madison and the Creation of the American Republic* (Glenview, Ill.: Little, Brown, 1990); and Lance Banning, *The Sacred Fire of Liberty: James Madison and the Founding of the Federal Republic* (Ithaca, N.Y.: Cornell University Press, 1995).

11. Especially by congressmen and other insiders in New York who hurried cash and agents to the farther reaches of the Union to gobble up outstanding state certificates before their holders were aware how much they would increase in value.

12. Speech of February 18, 1790, in *The Papers of James Madison* (hereafter *PJM*), ed. William T. Hutchinson et al. (Chicago: University of Chicago Press, 1962–), 13:48–49.

13. Dumas Malone, *Jefferson and His Time*, 6 vols. (Boston: Little, Brown, 1948–1981); Merrill D. Peterson, *Thomas Jefferson and the New Nation: A Biography* (London: Oxford University Press, 1970). Jefferson was forty-seven; Washington himself was only fifty-five. Our mental images are formed by late-life portraits of the founders, but they were vigorous young men during their most productive years.

14. This oversimplifies some cloudy bargaining and intricate maneuvers. The most recent discussion is Kenneth R. Bowling, *The Creation of Washington, D.C.: The Idea and Location of the American Capital* (Fairfax, Va.: George Mason University Press, 1991), chap. 7: "The Compromise of 1790."

15. Madison's speech on the national bank, February 2, 1791, in *PJM*, 13:373–81; Jefferson's "Opinion on the Constitutionality of a National Bank," February 15, 1791, in *The Works of Thomas Jefferson*, ed. Paul Leicester Ford, 12 vols. (New York: G. P. Putnam's Sons, 1904), 5:284–89. The constitutional debate between the parties is the subject of chapter 2.

16. Bank stock could be paid for one-fourth in specie and three-fourths in government bonds. Madison came as close to outrage as it was possible for him to do in response to the "scramble for . . . public plunder" attendant on the opening of the national bank, writing Jefferson, "My imagination will not attempt to set bounds to the daring depravity of the times. The stock-jobbers will become the praetorian band of the government, at once its tools and its tyrants; bribed by its largesses, and overawing it by clamors and combinations" (*PJM*, 14:43, 69).

17. This characterization of Hamilton's course came in an interview of Madison by Nicholas P. Trist, September 27, 1834. But compare Jefferson's late-life discussion in his preface to his "Anas," *Works of Thomas Jefferson*, 1:167–83.

18. Lance Banning, *The Jeffersonian Persuasion: Evolution of a Party Ideology* (Ithaca, N.Y.: Cornell University Press, 1978) traces the development of party thought. See especially pp. 153–55 and chap. 6.

19. Important discussions of the configurations of the first party struggle include Richard Buel Jr., *Securing the Revolution: Ideology in American Politics, 1789–1815* (Ithaca, N.Y.: Cornell University Press, 1972); David Hackett Fischer, *The Revolution of American Conservatism* (New York: Harper & Row, 1965), app. 1; and Paul Goodman, "The First American Party System," in *The American Party Systems: Stages of Political Development*, ed. William Nesbit Chambers and Walter Dean Burnham (Oxford: Oxford University Press, 1967), 56–89. Among many state and local studies, two have been especially influential: Paul Goodman, *The Democratic-Republicans of Massachusetts* (Cambridge, Mass.: Harvard University Press, 1964), and Alfred F. Young, *The Democratic Republicans of New York* (Chapel Hill: University of North Carolina Press, 1967).

20. See Gordon S. Wood, *The Radicalism of the American Revolution* (New York: Knopf, 1992), and, for the division between friends of liberty and friends of order, Thomas P. Slaughter, *The Whiskey Rebellion: Frontier Epilogue to the American Revolution* (New York: Oxford University Press, 1986).

21. Contrasting attitudes toward popular political involvement are the subject of chapter 3.

22. See my *Sacred Fire of Liberty* for an extended argument that prevailing scholarly opinions do not properly distinguish Madison's objectives from those of other advocates of the Constitution and thus suggest that Madison shifted course in the years after 1789 more radically than I believe he did.

23. My discussion of Republican political economy prefers McCoy, *The Elusive Republic*, to Joyce Appleby, *Capitalism and a New Social Order: The Republican Vision of the 1790s* (New York: New York University Press, 1984), but draws on Appleby as well for its insistence on the forward-looking, revolutionary enterprise of freeing individuals from hierarchical restraints and creating a harmonious society of self-directing equals. For an argument that revolutionary (or Republican) demands for public virtue seldom sought a selfless, sacrificial dedication to a larger public good but did expect a self-assertive, vigilant participation in a politics of equals, see Lance Banning, "Some Second Thoughts on Virtue and the Course of Revolutionary Thinking," in *Conceptual Change and the Constitution*, ed. Terence Ball and J. G. A. Pocock (Lawrence: University Press of Kansas, 1988), 194–212. For the debate among historians about the character and sources of Republican ideas, see further Lance Banning, "The Republican Hypothesis: Retrospect and Prospect," in *The Republican Synthesis Revisited: Essays in Honor of George Athan Billias*, ed. Milton M. Klein et al. (Worchester,

Mass.: American Antiquarian Society, 1992), 91–117; Banning, "Jefferson-ian Ideology Revisited: Liberal and Classical Ideas in the New American Republic," *William and Mary Quarterly*, 3rd ser., 43 (1986): 3–19; and the sources cited in these two essays.

24. See the Report of July 29 in *Journals of the Continental Congress. 1774–1789*, ed. Worthington Chauncy Ford et al., 34 vols. (Washington, D.C.: U.S. Government Printing Office, 1904–1937), 22:435–37, 432, and Morris to John Jay, July 13, 1781, quoted in Ferguson, *Power of the Purse*, 123–24.

25. The quotation is from the last "Continentalist" essay, published on July 4, 1782, just days before Morris's report, but see also the letters to an un-known recipient (undated), to James Duane (September 3, 1780), and to Morris (April 30, 1781), *PAH*, 3:106; 2:234–51, 400–18, 604–35.

26. Ferguson, in *The Power of the Purse*, was the first to see that the Mor-ris nationalists understood and wished to reproduce "the role of funded debt and national bank in stabilizing the regime founded in Britain after the rev-olution of 1689" (289–90). See further Banning, *The Jeffersonian Persuasion*, 126–40; McCoy, *The Elusive Republic*; John M. Murrin, "The Great Inver-sion, or Court versus Country: A Comparison of the Revolution Settlements in England (1688–1721) and America (1776–1816)," in *Three British Revo-lutions: 1641, 1688, 1776*, ed. J. G. A. Pocock (Princeton, N.J.: Princeton Uni-versity Press, 1980), 368–453; and Ralph Ketcham, *Presidents above Party: The First American Presidency, 1789–1829* (Chapel Hill: University of North Car-olina Press, 1984), 31–38 and chap. 10.

27. For the response to Morris, with whom Madison broke on the issue in 1783, see Banning, *The Sacred Fire of Liberty*, 29–33. Note particularly the re-sistance at that time and in 1790, by Madison as well as others, to "a perma-nent debt supported by a permanent general revenue"—that is, to any fund-ing system that worked in practice as Great Britain's did. Morris's proposal made no provision for retirement of the principal of the debt, and Hamilton's original plan offered more an illusion than a solid scheme along these lines. Indeed, as a security to creditors against early redemptions, which would have threatened the value of their notes, he would have limited redemptions to 1 percent per year and set aside for this purpose only surplus revenue from the post office. But, of course, it was not necessary to the system that the debt should actually be paid, only that the interest should be guaranteed.

28. Its stabilizing role is a central theme for J. H. Plumb, *The Growth of Political Stability in England, 1675–1725* (London: Macmillan, 1967).

29. The literature on British opposition thinking and its influence in America is now too vast to cite, but see, as a beginning, J. G. A. Pocock, "Machiavelli, Harrington, and English Political Ideologies in the Eighteenth

Century," *William and Mary Quarterly* 22 (1965): 549–63, and *The Machiavellian Moment: Florentine Political Thought and the Atlantic Republican Tradition* (Princeton, N.J.: Princeton University Press, 1975); Isaac Kramnick, *Bolingbroke and His Circle: The Politics of Nostalgia in the Age of Walpole* (Cambridge, Mass.: Harvard University Press, 1968); and H. T. Dickinson, *Liberty and Property: Political Ideology in Eighteenth-Century Britain* (New York: Holmes & Meier, 1977).

30. By the time of the Revolution, five-eighths of British revenues were required to service the debt, ordinary people were subjected to taxes (mostly excise taxes) as high as anywhere in Europe, and great political economists such as David Hume and Adam Smith were as worried by the debt as were the lesser lights who filled the opposition prints.

31. The masterworks on the enormous influence of this thinking on the Revolution are Pocock, *The Machiavellian Moment*; Bernard Bailyn, *The Ideological Origins of the American Revolution* (Cambridge, Mass.: Harvard University Press, 1967); and Gordon S. Wood, *The Creation of the American Republic, 1776–1787* (Chapel Hill: University of North Carolina Press, 1969). For introductions to the fuller literature, see Robert Shalhope, "Toward a Republican Synthesis: The Emergence of an Understanding of Republicanism in American Historiography," *William and Mary Quarterly*, 3rd ser., 29 (1972): 49–80; Shalhope, "Republicanism and Early American Historiography," *William and Mary Quarterly*, 3rd ser., 39 (1982): 334–56; Peter S. Onuf, "Reflections on the Founding: Constitutional Historiography in Bicentennial Perspective," *William and Mary Quarterly*, 3rd ser., 45 (1989): 341–375; and Banning, "The Republican Hypothesis," 91–117.

32. *Works of Thomas Jefferson*, 7:138–39.

33. Curtis P. Nettels, *The Emergence of a National Economy, 1775–1815* (New York: Harper & Row, 1962), 48–49, estimates that the deficit in trade with Britain in the three years after the peace was more than £5,000,000. Scholars disagree about the breadth, the depth, and the duration of the downturn, but later work accords with Nettels's, which remains the standard study, that it was sharper and more general than older, "progressive" scholarship suggested. See John J. McCusker and Russell R. Menard, *The Economy of British America, 1606–1789* (Chapel Hill: University of North Carolina Press, 1985), 367–77, and Richard B. Morris, *The Forging of the Union, 1781–1789* (New York: Harper & Row, 1987), chap. 6.

34. Nettles, *The Emergence of a National Economy*, 72–75; Frederick W. Marks III, *Independence on Trial: Foreign Affairs and the Making of the Constitution* (Baton Rouge: Louisiana State University Press, 1973), 80–82; Cathy D. Matson and Peter S. Onuf, *A Union of Interests: Political and Economic Thought in Revolutionary America* (Lawrence: University Press of Kansas,

1990), chap. 2; and Forrest McDonald, *Novus Ordo Seclorum: The Intellectual Origins of the Constitution* (Lawrence: University Press of Kansas, 1985), 102–6.

35. I lean most heavily on McCoy, *The Elusive Republic*, especially chap. 1, and Pocock, *The Machiavellian Moment*.

36. Albert O. Hirschman, *The Passions and the Interests: Political Arguments for Capitalism before Its Triumph* (Princeton, N.J.: Princeton University Press, 1977), and the introductory essay in Istvan Hont and Michael Ignatieff, eds., *Wealth and Virtue: The Shaping of Political Economy in the Scottish Enlightenment* (Cambridge: Cambridge University Press, 1983).

37. Among the English, the most notorious example was Bernard Mandeville, *The Fable of the Bees: or Private Vices, Public Benefits* (London: J. Roberts, 1714). Far more moderate in tone but also relatively unrestrained in their defense of commerce were David Hume's influential essays "Of Commerce," "Of Luxury," and "Of Refinement in the Arts," published in 1752 and available in *Essays: Moral, Political, and Literary*, ed. Eugene F. Miller (Indianapolis: Liberty Classics, 1985).

38. Adam Smith, *An Inquiry into the Nature and Causes of the Wealth of Nations*, ed. Edwin Cannan (New York: Random House, 1937), 734–40. See, more broadly, McCoy's superb discussion of Smith and other Scots, *The Elusive Republic*, 19–21, 35–40, and McDonald, *Novus Ordo Seclorum*, chap. 4.

39. Smith devoted much of book 4 of *Wealth of Nations* to a condemnation of policies designed "to enrich a great nation rather by trade and manufactures than by the improvement and cultivation of land, rather by the industry of the towns than by that of the country" (591).

40. For unqualified defenses of commercialization in the resolutions of public meetings and the writings of William Barton, David Daggett, and William Vans Murray, see McCoy, *The Elusive Republic*, 96–100, 118–19, and Matson and Onuf, *A Union of Interests*, 91–97.

41. Madison's movement toward support of thoroughgoing constitutional reform was gradual and complex, and a full, persuasive demonstration of this point cannot be offered in this brief a compass. I have attempted it in *The Sacred Fire of Liberty*, 58–75.

42. See also McCoy, *The Elusive Republic*, 121–32.

43. Madison to Jefferson, March 18, 1786, *PJM*, 8:502.

44. Madison to James Monroe, August 7, 1785, *PJM*, 8:333–36.

45. September 7, 1784, enclosing Madison to Jefferson, August 20, 1784, *PJM*, 8:113–14, 104–8.

46. This was first clearly recognized and is still superbly explained in McCoy, *The Elusive Republic*, 121–32.

47. Query 19 of *Notes on the State of Virginia*, written in 1781–1782 and carefully read by Madison no later than the early fall of 1785.

48. See his *National Gazette* essays on "Republican Distribution of Citizens" (March 3, 1792) and "Fashion" (March 20, 1792) in *PJM*, 14:244–46, 257–59.

49. Speech of April 8, 1789, and supporting speeches of April 21, April 25, and May 4 in *PJM*, 12:64–66, 97–103, 109–13, 125–30. Defeated in 1789, Madison revived this effort twice again, in 1790 and 1794, before a treaty with Britain forbade such measures for the next ten years. In 1790 and 1794, he was defeated, in part, by Hamilton's determined opposition.

50. Madison's speeches of the early 1790s are the fullest sources for this thinking, which was also developed in his *National Gazette* essays on "Parties," "Republican Distribution of Citizens," and "Fashion," together with his "Political Observations" of April 20, 1795, *PJM*, 14:197–98, 244–46, 257–59, 15:511–34. For Jefferson, see Merrill Peterson, "Thomas Jefferson and Commercial Policy, 1783–1793," *William and Mary Quarterly*, 3rd ser., 22 (1965): 584–610. On the Jeffersonians in power, McCoy, *The Elusive Republic*, chaps. 8–10, and Banning, *The Jeffersonian Persuasion*, chap. 10, may be supplemented with J. C. A. Stagg, "James Madison and the Coercion of Great Britain: Canada, the West Indies, and the War of 1812," *William and Mary Quarterly*, 3rd ser., 38 (1981): 3–34, and Donald R. Hickey, "American Trade Restrictions during the War of 1812," *Journal of American History* 68 (1981): 517–38.

51. See especially the Report on Manufactures, *PAH*, 10:287–90, which McCoy, in *The Elusive Republic*, rightly calls "Hamilton's answer to Madison's defense of commercial discrimination" (150). Hamilton's indebtedness to Hume, the great Scottish philosopher, historian, and essayist, was well established in Miller, *Alexander Hamilton*, 46–51, and in Stourzh, *Hamilton and the Idea of Republican Government*, 70–75. For the influence of the Scottish mercantilist James Steuart (*An Inquiry into the Principles of Political Oeconomy* [1767]), see McDonald, *Novus Ordo Seclorum*, 119–28, 135–42.

52. Report on Manufactures, *PAH*, 10:255–56.

53. Report on Manufactures, *PAH*, 10:230–40.

54. John R. Nelson, "Alexander Hamilton and American Manufacturing: A Reexamination," *Journal of American History* 65 (1979): 971–95; Nelson, *Liberty and Property: Political Economy and Policymaking in the New Nation, 1789–1812* (Baltimore: Johns Hopkins University Press, 1987), 81–90; and Young, *The Democratic Republicans of New York*.

55. Nelson, *Liberty and Property*, 90–96; Murrin, "The Great Inversion," 412, 419–21; and sources cited by both.

56. Here, without accepting their interpretive positions, I draw especially on Appleby, *Capitalism and a New Social Order*; Steven Watts, *The Republic*

Reborn: War and the Making of Liberal America, 1790–1820 (Baltimore: Johns Hopkins University Press, 1987); and Michael Durey, "Thomas Paine's Apostles: Radical Émigrés and the Triumph of Jeffersonian Republicanism," *William and Mary Quarterly* 44 (1987): 661–86. Years ago, in *Tom Paine and Revolutionary America* (New York: Oxford University Press, 1976), Eric Foner suggested that the author of "Common Sense" and many of the artisans to whom he most appealed were uniquely sympathetic to *both* of the great transformations of the age: popular participation in political affairs *and* the advent of an advanced market economy. The influence of this thinking, both democratic and profoundly pro-developmental, has become even clearer in more recent works, such as Lawrence A. Peskin, "How the Republicans Learned to Love Manufacturing: The First Parties and the 'New Economy,'" *Journal of the Early Republic* 22 (spring 2002): 235–62, and Andrew Shankman, *Crucible of American Democracy: The Struggle to Fuse Egalitarianism and Capitalism in Jeffersonian Pennsylvania* (Lawrence: University Press of Kansas, 2004).

57. Jefferson to William H. Crawford, *Works of Thomas Jefferson*, 11:537–39.

58. Madison, who had been willing even in 1789 to protect manufactories that had already emerged, though not to foster new ones, now specifically endorsed protection for some "manufacturing establishments . . . of the more complicated kind" (quoted in McCoy, *The Elusive Republic*, 245). Jefferson was more reluctant. See his letter to Benjamin Austin, January 9, 1816, *Works of Thomas Jefferson*, 11:502–5.

59. Suggestively, in his last important act as president, Madison vetoed the bill providing for internal improvement, insisting that a constitutional amendment was required.

60. Shankman's study of the Pennsylvanians is particularly instructive for its insistence on the essential differences between Hamilton's own vision and the national republicanism (later Whiggery) that was beginning to emerge during these years.

• 2 •

The First Constructions of the Constitution

$\mathscr{B}$y the spring of 1792, just three years after the new federal government had gone into effect, its greatest champions were deeply and increasingly divided over how it should be shaped. The reasons for their conflict were complex and utterly profound, stretching from the start—and ever more apparently as both sides tried to mobilize the public—over nearly every aspect of the nation's public life. Clashing views about the foreign, economic, and financial policies best suited for the new republic welled from deeply different regional perspectives and from radically opposing lessons drawn from the experience and the inheritance of thought from eighteenth-century Britain. Contrasting attitudes toward popular participation hinted at fundamentally contending visions of the nature of a sound republic. So, however, did the rapidly emerging parties' differing conceptions of the nature of the federal union and a sound interpretation of the document on which it rested. The infant Constitution may have been the longest step toward defining how liberty could be secured in an extended, federal republic, but it did not by any means resolve this question. The workability and wisdom of the novel federal system conceived by the Constitutional Convention was the central issue in the national debate over whether the Constitution should be ratified or not. The ambiguities inherent in the constitutional division of authority continued to divide the founders through the rest of their careers.

Through much of the twentieth century, as "states' rights" were discredited and national power grew, the finest scholarship about the founding tended to neglect its federal dimensions, which also seemed of little interest to the nation or its courts. Nevertheless, in the years surrounding the adoption of the Constitution, federalism seemed as crucial as republicanism to the aspirations of the revolutionary generation—as crucial and as problematic. These master concepts were, indeed, inseparably connected by a general agreement that the great experiment in liberty—that is, in the creation of a governmental system grounded exclusively on popular consent and popular control but at the same time offering firm securities for individual rights—could not succeed without a continental union yet would just as surely fail in a consolidated or unitary national republic. Continental union seemed to nearly everyone the only guarantee that North America would not become another Europe, where a multitude of rival states or small confederations, always on the edge of war, would arm themselves with standing military forces, powerful executives, large debts, high taxes, and other unrepublican equipage. A single national government, however, seemed hardly less consistent with protection for the rights of all or with the sorts of bonds between the rulers and the ruled that characterized a genuine republic.

The eighteenth-century British Empire was a working federal system, in practice though not in theory. Judged by the prosperity and power of the empire, the system was successful. But many British politicians were convinced that it was failing. Setting out to fix what may not have needed fixing, they tightened supervision of the colonies and, after 1763, attempted parliamentary taxation. The empire shattered on its inability to solve or even to define the federal problem: How might political authority be safely, effectively, and lastingly divided between the central and subordinate governments? In the end, the colonies would fight rather than concede that there were no definable limits to parliamentary sovereignty. The English would fight rather than concede that parliament's authority was "constitutionally" constrained by the subordinate authority of the colonial assemblies. As Americans declared their independence, they concluded from the conflict with a distant, unresponsive central government that liberty must be secured by written constitutions and a union carefully restricted to a narrow range of general concerns. Ten years later, nevertheless, the new American union was itself in danger of collapse over the difficulties posed by its own initial effort to resolve this problem.

Early on, to put it quickly, the federal riddle seemed to have a fairly obvious solution. As Thomas Jefferson expressed it, "To make us one nation as to foreign concerns and keep us distinct in domestic ones gives the outline of the proper division of powers between the general and particular governments."[1] The Union would be a firm and perpetual league of friendship between the several new republics, whose Continental Congress would concern itself almost exclusively with war and international relations. Surprisingly little systematic thought was given to the matter. The Articles of Confederation, not even ratified until 1781, did little more than formalize the institutions and authority that had evolved in practice in the years since 1774.[2]

By 1781, however, it was clear to the majority of national leaders that the Articles of Confederation were seriously flawed, and by the middle 1780s, even relatively localistic leaders thought the Union was in crisis. Constitutional reform would not have taken the distinctive shape it took if many of those leaders had not been disgusted with the policies adopted in the several states during a sharp postwar depression. The Constitution was deliberately designed to correct the democratic errors that many of its framers thought had been committed in the states.[3] But constitutional reform would not have come about at all if the Confederation had been able to confront the economic downturn, pay its debts, and handle other problems—if many, for that matter, had not believed that the Union was in imminent danger of dissolution and even that the failure of the republican Revolution could follow the collapse of the Union.

Even at this point, the reach of national consensus seems as striking as any of the arguments that would ensue. The Constitutional Convention easily achieved a firm agreement that the current federal arrangement was inherently and irredeemably defective: A sovereignty over sovereigns, a general government requiring independent action by the states to execute its measures, would have to be replaced by one deriving more directly from the people and possessing independent means of compelling obedience to its commands.[4] Still, the Constitutional Convention worked within a general agreement also on the powers or responsibilities that ought to be in federal hands, and these were generally conceded to be relatively few: an independent power of taxation, regulation of the country's trade, the powers vested in the general Congress by the old Confederation, and a handful of additional responsibilities requiring general supervision. Accordingly, a reconstructed central government, responsible for a limited range of general concerns, was placed atop a confederation of republics. Indeed, I would suggest, the framers' consciousness that they were framing a general government of specific and limited powers is the best explanation even for their greatest mistake: their unanimous decision not to frame a bill of rights. It just did not seem necessary to forbid the federal government from acting on a range of subjects over which it had been granted no authority to start with.

Original understandings are, in most respects, a troublesome, contentious issue. Remarkably, however, few participants on either side of the impressive national debate about adoption of the Constitution broke from the agreement that a firm, effective union was essential to the liberty, prosperity, and happiness of the United States, while a consolidated national government would prove destructive to them all. *The Federalist* was vitally concerned to demonstrate that every power granted to the central government was at once essential and guarded as carefully as reason could require against the possibility of abuse, that the Constitution was not so much an addition of new powers to the general government as a means of rendering its current powers more effective, and that the mass of powers granted to the central government would not endanger the residual rights of the people and the states. The finest writers on the other side, "Brutus" and "The Federal Farmer," acknowledged that the document did not create a unitary system and admitted that the Union needed to be strengthened. Their argument with "Publius" was over whether any system structured as the new one was and armed not only with the powers actually enumerated in the Constitution but also with the power to enact such other laws as might be "necessary and proper" to carry the enumerated powers into action would continue to be limited for any length of time. There can be little doubt that people ratified the Constitution understanding, as Virginia put it, "that every power not granted thereby remains with [the people]" and, as New York added, "that those clauses in the said Constitution which declare that Congress shall not have or exercise certain powers do not imply that Congress is entitled to any powers not given by the said Constitution, but such clauses are to be construed either as exceptions to certain specified powers or as inserted merely for greater caution."[5]

But even a Constitution many times as long as this one was could not have answered every question. Thus, as soon as the first new Congress turned to the creation of a presidential cabinet, a puzzle was immediately apparent. The document was clear about who had the power of appointing major officers of state: the president, acting with the consent of the Senate. The Constitution said nothing, however, about who had the power to dismiss these great executive officials. Implications and interpretations were impossible to do without. And two years later, in 1791, when Alexander Hamilton proposed the creation of a national bank, James Madison, who had collaborated with him on *The Federalist*, initiated an enduring argument between proponents of strict and broad constructions of the "sweeping clauses."[6] Indeed, with a single, partial exception—the Alien and Sedition Acts of 1798—every constitutional debate within the founders' lifetimes centered not on different understandings of the Bill of Rights, as most contemporary controversies do, but on a sound construction of these "general clauses" and the constitutional limits of federal power. Hamilton, followed by the Marshall court, effectively rebutted Thomas Jefferson's insistence that measures were not "necessary" unless an enumerated power could not be carried into effect without them.[7] Still, neither Hamilton nor Marshall ever really answered Madison's original objection: If "necessary" means no more than "useful," what is to prevent a chain of reasoning that may completely overturn the constitutional enumeration of limited powers, justifying any measure if it can be said, however distantly, to aid toward the accomplishment of some enumerated end? Nor was everyone willing to agree that all such questions should be settled by the courts. Andrew Jackson stood with several of the founders when he said, supposedly, that he would perform his executive duties according to his own reading of the Constitution, not John Marshall's.

Suppose, moreover, that all three branches of the federal government should unite in "a deliberate, palpable, and dangerous exercise of . . . powers not granted" by the Constitution, which was the problem that Madison and Jefferson perceived in the legislation of 1798. In that event, Virginia and Kentucky (Madison and Jefferson) said the states, which were the parties to the constitutional compact, should interpose to take "the necessary and proper measures . . . for maintaining unimpaired the authorities, rights, and liberties reserved to the states respectively, or to the people."[8] But then, again, interposition led in no great time to nullification and secession. Even Madison, perhaps the greatest constitutional theorist the country has ever produced, was never able to sit securely between the horns that seem to stick us either with disunionism (and the tyranny of local majorities) or with what we have come to call an imperial judiciary (and the tyranny of unelected, unresponsive judges).

The understandings of the founders often prove impossible to capture. Different founders disagreed. A single founder might take different stands at different points.[9] And even where the founders' stands *can* be discovered, we may still deny that their positions should control our own. It pays us, nevertheless, to probe the founders' views. For, on the reasons why our system should be only partly national in nature, on the intimate relationship between federalism and republicanism, and on the ways in which a federal division of authority can be maintained, we have yet to find Americans who thought so deeply or so well.

In 1789, the triumph of the Constitution was conditional and incomplete. Two states, North Carolina and Rhode Island, had rejected the reform. Several others had approved it only on the understanding that amendments would immediately be framed. The close and sharp division over its adoption had intensified a feeling, in its friends and foes alike, that liberty itself might stand or fall on the decisions of the next few years. Supporters of the Constitution thought that it had saved the Union from the danger of a speedy dissolution and had armed that union, after years of ineffectuality, with powers equal to its duties. But even its most ardent champions were painfully aware that every measure of the first new Congress would establish precedents for everything to come and that the Constitutional Convention had reserved for them a number of decisions needed to complete the system: creation of judicial and executive departments, not to mention resolution of the problems that had wrecked the old Confederation.[10] Even its most ardent champions, moreover, differed more than they were currently aware about the policies that would be necessary to restore the nation's health, the character of the regime created by the Constitution, and the strategies most likely to secure it.

At the Constitutional Convention, Alexander Hamilton had candidly confessed that, if the nation's sentiments did not forbid it, he would favor abolition of the states or turning them into administrative districts of a national republic.[11] James Madison, by contrast, searched from the beginning of deliberations for a "middle ground" between excessive "independence" for the states and a complete consolidation.[12] Hamilton and Madison were able to collaborate effectively in their magnificent defense of the convention's work because they both believed that the completed Constitution was a safe and necessary remedy for pressing national ills. Beneath their large agreements, nonetheless—beyond the topics that they needed to pursue in order to defend the Constitution—the authors of *The Federalist* had vastly different visions of the sort of nation the United States should be, contrasting attitudes about the document itself, and different ideas about the policies most likely to attach the people to it.

Hamilton, as we have seen, intended over time to arm the infant government with the financial, economic, and administrative tools that would permit it to compete with European empires on the Europeans' terms. He hoped to overcome endemic localism, which he always saw as the outstanding danger to the Union, by detaching vital portions of the nation's natural leadership from their connections with the states and binding them, by solid ties of interest, to the central government's success. No one's preferences, he told the great convention, differed more than his from the completed Constitution. He supported it because he calculated, privately, that it would make it possible for an efficient administration to promote prosperity, secure the people's loyalty, and move the country gradually toward greater centralization.[13]

Madison, by contrast, understood the Constitution as an instrument by which America could long avoid the European institutions Hamilton associated with a modern state.[14] His politics had always been affected more than some contemporaries saw (and more than modern scholarship has generally perceived) by early revolutionary condemnations of the British system of administration and finance, which Hamilton, as secretary of the treasury, would replicate as far as he was able. As the Constitutional Convention closed, Madison, as well as Hamilton, was doubtful that the reconstructed government could actually correct the failings of the old Confederation.[15] But as they wrote *The Federalist*, Madison was more successful than his colleague in concluding that the Constitution was a better document than he had thought when it was signed—indeed, that in the Constitution's complex, partly federal features, the convention had contrived the best expedient that human ingenuity had yet discovered for securing liberty completely. Madison did not believe that it was possible (much less desirable) to integrate America in imitation of Great Britain; its citizens were too diverse, too nearly equal, and too little deferential. Unlike Hamilton, an immigrant who would dismiss complaints about the regional inequities of his designs as simply selfish and divisive, Madison, who was distinctively Virginian in his thinking, was convinced that the United States could hold together only if its leaders consciously displayed a spirit of mutual accommodation. Certainly, he would accommodate demands for the addition of a bill of rights, not least because there was a good deal in the hopes and fears of sensible opponents of the Constitution to which he was, in fact, quite sympathetic.

"Brutus," Madison confessed, not long before agreeing to unite with Hamilton in their defense of the reform, struck plausibly at the foundations of the Constitution.[16] "Although the government reported by the convention does not go to a perfect and entire consolidation," "Brutus" wrote, "yet it approaches so near to it that it must, if executed, certainly and infallibly terminate in it." The central government was granted "absolute and uncontrollable power" over "every object to which it extends," including power to enact such laws as might be "necessary and proper" to carry its enumerated powers into execution, and "the powers of the general legislature extend to every case that is of the least importance." Federal laws and treaties would be the supreme laws of the land, binding every judge throughout the country, and there would be no need for any action by the states to carry them into effect. Certainly, the federal taxing powers would extend to every object whatever since Congress would itself determine whether this tax or the other was "for the general welfare." In no great time, accordingly, the states would be "annihilated, except so far as they are barely necessary to the organization of the general government." But "a free republic," "Brutus" argued, could not "succeed over a country of such immense extent":

> If the people are to give their assent to the laws, by persons chosen
> and appointed by them, the manner of the choice and number cho-

sen must be such as to possess, be disposed, and consequently qualified to declare the sentiments of the people; for if they do not know or are not disposed to speak the sentiments of the people, the people do not govern, but the sovereignty is in a few. . . . In a large extended country, it is impossible to have a representation possessing the sentiments and of integrity to declare the minds of the people without having it so numerous and unwieldy as to be subject in great measure to the inconveniency of a [direct] democratic government.

In a genuine republic, too, the laws were executed "by the people turning out to aid the magistrate," not by military force. The people would do this, however, only if the government was "so constructed as to have the confidence, respect, and affection of the people," which would not be likely in a country as extensive as the United States. The people could not know their rulers, follow their proceedings, change them with facility, or unite with citizens in distant sections of the country to force a change, nor could their representatives be thoroughly familiar with local conditions and needs. Without the confidence of the people, there would be no way to make the laws effective "but by establishing an armed force to execute the laws at the point of the bayonet."[17]

"A fair and equal representation," another Antifederalist observed, "is that in which the interests, feelings, opinions, and views of the people are collected in such manner as they would be were the people all assembled." It was dishonest to assure the people that they could choose their rulers "if they cannot, in the nature of things, choose men from among themselves and genuinely like themselves." But this could never be the case in an American legislature smaller than a mob. Legislators would inevitably be chosen from the four or five thousand natural aristocrats in the country: state governors or judges, members of the general Congress, state senators, army and militia officers, large property owners, and eminent professionals. The huge variety among the people would not be mirrored among legislators whose sympathies and associations would be entirely with other members of the national elite. The members of the legislature would inevitably be "too far removed from the people in general to sympathize with them, and too few to communicate with them." The people would be governed by an unresponsive few.[18]

Madison, though often understood too narrowly as the ratification contest's most determined champion of large republics, was not insensitive to these concerns. Even in his famous essay arguing that large republics are superior to small ones in their capacity "to secure the public good and private rights against the danger of" majority factions, he admitted that "there is a mean on both sides of which inconveniences will be found to lie." If districts were too large, the representative might well be unfamiliar with the people's "local circumstances and lesser interests." If they were small, he might be "unduly attached to these, and too little fit to comprehend and pursue great and national objects. The federal Constitution forms a happy combination in this respect—the great and aggregate interests being referred to the national, the local and particular to the state legislatures."[19]

Madison was not, in truth, an advocate of large republics simply defined. He argued, rather, that "the larger the society, provided it lie within a practicable sphere, the more duly capable it will be of self-government. And happily for the *republican cause*, the practicable sphere may be carried to a very great extent by a judicious modification and mixture of the *federal principle*."[20] In *Federalist* 39, he offered the most impressive contemporary analysis of the unprecedented blend of "federal" and "national" features in the Constitution, and he was centrally concerned throughout these essays to persuade opponents that this novel compound could endure. "In the compound republic of America," he wrote, "the power surrendered by the people is first divided between two distinct governments and then the portion allotted to each subdivided among distinct and separate departments." Within each set of governments, the different branches would be chosen sometimes more and sometimes less directly by the people, and this would guarantee a due concern for both their short- and their long-term needs. The state and general governments would each be charged exclusively with the responsibilities that each was best equipped to handle, guarding the society against the threat of unresponsive rulers. The state and general governments would each control the other "at the same time that each will be controlled by itself"—and by the sovereign people. As long as that common master continued to be fit for freedom, Madison believed, future generations would continue to enjoy as much self-government as human nature would allow.[21]

But once (and if) the people have approved a Constitution properly dividing state and general responsibilities, will they really be inclined and able to ensure that this division will be lasting? Amendments, Antifederalists insisted, were essential to confine the federal government within a limited sphere, and despite initial reservations, Madison, the leader of the House of Representatives in 1789, decided that amendments could be framed that would accommodate their fears without affecting a proper division of responsibilities and powers.[22] Drafting the amendments himself, he offered mostly what he understood as "additional securities"—redundant guarantees—against the possibility of federal intrusions into matters over which the federal government had not been granted any power to begin with (although he also sponsored an amendment barring *state* infringements of the most essential rights and one ensuring that the federal House of Representatives would be enlarged). State preserves as well as individual rights received additional protection. Madison was careful to insert provisions that became the Ninth Amendment, without which, he believed, an effort to enumerate essential rights might prove more dangerous than safe: "The enumeration in the Constitution of certain rights shall not be construed to deny or disparage others retained by the people." The Tenth Amendment, in his view, encapsulated the agreement reached in the course of the recent national debate: "The powers not delegated to the United States by the Constitution, nor prohibited by it to the states, are reserved to the states respectively, or to the people."

Already, nonetheless, events had shown that even an amended Constitution could not answer every question. The episode, indeed, was surely one of many reasons why Madison and other congressmen refused to write a tenth amendment that would have declared that powers not "expressly" granted were reserved, which was the language of the Articles of Confederation.

On May 19, 1789, three months before the House felt free to turn to constitutional amendments, Madison had moved for the creation of executive departments whose heads could be dismissed by the president acting alone. William Loughton Smith, a South Carolina congressman, objected that impeachment was the only method of removing officers mentioned in the Constitution, while Theodorick Bland, Madison's Virginia colleague, believed that the requirement of concurrence by the Senate in appointments might imply that its concurrence should be necessary also for removals. Madison, who was determined to defend the separation of powers, responded first that he believed the Constitution's silence on the matter left it to congressional discretion.[23] On second thought, however, he retracted this idea as ill-digested. A sound interpretation of the Constitution, he now remarked, was certainly among the most important tasks that early congresses would face. Their decisions would inevitably "become the permanent exposition of the Constitution; and on a permanent exposition of the Constitution will depend the genius and character of the whole government."[24] Nor could Congress simply leave such matters to the courts, as some of his colleagues suggested. In the ordinary course of governmental operations, it was true, "the exposition of the laws and Constitution" would of course devolve on this branch:

> But I beg to know upon what principle it can be contended that any one department draws from the Constitution greater powers than another in marking out the limits of the powers of the several departments. . . . If the constitutional boundary of either be brought into question, I do not see that any of these independent departments has more right than another to declare their sentiments on that point.

It was "incontrovertibly of as much importance" to the House as to any other branch of government, Madison maintained, "that the Constitution shall be preserved entire," and this, he now believed, would demand that Congress consider all "the great departments" in their constitutional relationship to one another, taking guidance from the fundamental principles that underpinned the charter. On this view, he argued now, the legislature could not constitutionally extend the limited exception to the executive power represented by the Senate's role in appointments, for this was dangerously at odds with the underlying principle of executive independence.[25]

To Madison, a sound interpretation of the Constitution might be hard to reach,[26] but the construction of the fundamental law was never to be merely instrumental to the ends that Congress wanted to pursue. The Constitution was the people's law, to be revered and not continually remolded by their servants.[27] Accordingly, it was by no means out of character for him, as the First Congress moved toward its conclusion, to object ferociously to Hamilton's proposal to create a national bank. This proposition, to be sure, went far toward showing him to what a very great degree the secretary of the treasury was seeking to reinstitute a British system of finance, an enterprise to which he had a multitude of deep objections. Thus, he opened his remarks of February 2, 1791, with substantive objections to the plan. But he was even more alarmed, he indicated, by the implications of the scheme for the interpretation of the Constitution, and we are well advised to take him at his word. It was a lifelong principle for Madison that "precedents of usurpation" have to be resisted on their first appearance, as they had been early in the Revolution, and the precedents that might be instituted by approval of the bank might well initiate the very process of degeneration that "Brutus" or the "Federal Farmer" had predicted.

Three years before, the leader of the House of Representatives had seen slight danger from increasing federal power. Nevertheless, he quite agreed with former Antifederalist opponents that a unitary national system would inevitably prove incompatible with freedom. A single national legislature, he observed, could never regulate the countless matters currently overseen by the states. Thus, a further concentration of authority in central hands would necessarily entail so great an increase of executive offices, responsibilities, and prerogatives as might transform the president into a monarch. The legislature, too, would steadily become more independent of the people since it would prove impossible to gather and enforce the genuine opinion of the people if they were deprived of the "local organs" through which their sentiments were currently conveyed.[28] However difficult the task, the maintenance of the federal division of responsibilities must never be abandoned, for there were no alternatives but "schism or consolidation; both of them bad, but the latter the worst, since it is the high road to monarchy, than which nothing worse, in the eye of republicans, could result from the anarchy implied in the former."[29]

The Constitution, Madison reminded the House, was "not a general grant, out of which particular powers are excepted—it is a grant of particular powers only, leaving the general mass in other hands. So it had been understood by its friends and its foes, and so it was to be interpreted." Nothing in the Constitution, he insisted, specifically empowered Congress to incorporate a national bank. A bank was not a borrowing of money, not an act for laying taxes, not an exercise of any power listed in the constitutional enumeration. And whether a bank was "necessary and proper" to carry the enumerated powers into action had to be determined by considering "its incidentality to an express authority," its intrinsic importance, and "the probability or improbability of its being left to construction." "Necessary and proper" meant "direct and incidental means" for carrying an enumerated power into execution. The clause was not to be interpreted in such a way as would give "an unlimited discretion to Congress"; it was "in fact merely declaratory of what would have resulted by unavoidable implication" if it had not been included at all, authorizing only such measures as were "*necessary* to the *end* and *incidental* to the *nature* of the specified power." To construe it as permitting *any* means that might "conduce" to execution of a delegated power, as suggested in the preamble to the bill, would destroy "the essential characteristic of a government . . . composed of limited and enumerated powers." "Mark the reasoning on which the validity of the bill depends," Madison objected:

> To borrow money is made the *end* and the accumulation of capitals *implied* as the *means*. The accumulation of capitals is then the *end* and a bank *implied* as the *means*. The bank is then the *end* and a charter of incorporation, a monopoly, capital punishment [for forging notes], etc. *implied* as the *means*.
> If implications thus remote and multiplied can be linked together, a chain may be formed that will reach every object of legislation, every object within the whole compass of political economy.

The power of incorporation, Madison insisted, could not be considered merely "an accessory or subaltern power to be deduced by implication . . .; it was in its nature a distinct, an independent and substantive prerogative," a power that he well remembered had been specifically rejected by the Constitutional Convention. The bank bill was a "usurpation," he maintained. It would establish precedents for an interpretation "levelling all the barriers which limit the powers of the general government" and destroying "the very character of the government" the Constitution created. It was "condemned by the exposition of the friends of the Constitution, whilst depending before the public; was condemned by the apparent intention of the parties which ratified the Constitution"; was condemned by the Ninth and Tenth Amendments; "and he hoped it would receive its final condemnation by the vote of the House."[30]

As the Constitution went into effect, George Washington depended more on Madison than on any other individual for advice about the Constitution.[31] Small wonder, then, that he immediately asked his cabinet for their opinions on the bank and Madison himself to draft a veto message. Attorney General Edmund Randolph and Secretary of State Thomas Jefferson agreed with their Virginia friend, the latter in a paper destined to become a great foundation for the doctrine of "strict construction" of the federal charter.

"To take a single step beyond" the Tenth Amendment, Jefferson wrote, "is to take possession of a boundless field of power, no longer susceptible of any definition." Incorporation of a bank was not an exercise of any delegated power and not an act consistent with a sound construction of "the general phrases." One of these permitted Congress "to lay taxes to provide for the general welfare"—not to lay taxes for any purpose it pleased and certainly not to do whatever it judged in the general welfare, for the last interpretation would render the enumeration absolutely useless. Clearly, too, the powers plainly granted Congress might all be carried into execution without a national bank, and the "necessary and proper" clause authorized "only the means which are 'necessary,' not those which are merely 'convenient.'" The contrary interpretation, again, would permit such "a latitude of construction . . . as to swallow up all the delegated powers" and transform the government from a limited one into an unlimited one. Properly constructed, the clause authorized only "those means without which the grant of [an enumerated] power would be nugatory." Mere "convenience," Jefferson insisted—even superior convenience—could not suffice to authorize Congress to impinge on state laws to the degree that the bank bill would do. "Nothing but a necessity invincible by any other means" could authorize such an act.[32]

Hamilton, who studied his colleagues' papers before preparing his own, made fairly easy work of Jefferson's opinion, which pushed a strict interpretation of federal authority a good deal farther than Madison had done. Jefferson, his colleague noted, read the "necessary and proper" clause as though it said "absolutely" or "indispensably" necessary. But

> such a construction would beget endless uncertainty & embarrassment. The cases must be palpable & extreme in which it could be pronounced with certainty that a measure was absolutely necessary, or one without which the exercise of a given power would be nugatory. There are few measures of any government which would stand so severe a test. To insist upon it would be to make the criterion of the exercise of any implied power a case of extreme necessity; which is rather a rule to justify the overleaping of the bounds of constitutional authority than to govern the ordinary exercise of it. . . . The *degree* in which a measure is necessary can never be a test of the *legal* right to adopt it. That must ever be a matter of opinion; and can only be a test of expediency. The *relation* between the *measure* and the *end*, between the *nature of the mean* employed towards the execution of a power and the object of that power, must be the criterion of constitutionality, not the more or less of *necessity* or *utility*. . . . The means by which national exigencies are to be provided for, national inconveniencies obviated, national prosperity promoted, are of such infinite variety, extent and complexity, that there must, of necessity, be great latitude of discretion in the selection & application of those means.

By all his opponents, Hamilton remarked, a corporation seemed to have been seen "as some great, independent, substantive thing—as a political end of peculiar magnitude & moment; whereas it is truly to be considered as a quality, capacity, or mean to an end," a means employed with regularity by every government whatever (and, without objection, by the new United States itself to create governments for the western territories). As Hamilton conceived it,

> Every power vested in a government is in its nature sovereign and includes by force of the term a right to employ all the means requisite and fairly applicable to the attainment of the ends of such power; and which are not precluded by restrictions and exceptions specified in the Constitution, or not immoral. Or not contrary to the essential ends of political society.

It was, he thought, "unquestionably incident to sovereign power to erect corporations, and consequently to that of the United States"—not, of course, for every purpose whatever but certainly "in relation to the objects entrusted to the management of the government." And in a paper several times as long as that of his colleagues, he went on to demonstrate "a natural and obvious relation between the institution of a bank and the objects of several of the enumerated powers."[33]

Washington may well have judged his secretary of the treasury the victor in this battle.[34] In comparison to Madison, Jefferson had made himself a fairly easy target, pushing his strict interpretation of federal authority so far as nearly to suggest that the Tenth Amendment did declare that powers not "expressly" delegated were reserved, a declaration that Madison himself had warned had bound the old Confederation so impossibly that Congress had been forced into repeated violations.[35] But Madison as well as Jefferson had characterized the power of incorporation as too great to have been left to implication, an opinion with which Washington was quite unlikely to agree. Hamilton, like Madison, admitted that the proper test for claims of an implicit power lay in the relationship between the measure (or the means) proposed and an enumerated power. Hamilton as well as Madison acknowledged that "the moment the literal meaning is departed from, there is a chance of error and abuse," and both of them expected many controverted cases. But Madison's elucidation of the test he had in mind was brief and fuzzy: the degree to which the means seemed clearly incidental and directly related to the end, the intrinsic importance of the measure, and "the probability or improbability" that authority for such a measure would have been left to implication and construction. These were not the sorts of tests that courts could reasonably employ—an observation that might not have troubled Madison, who did not believe (at that point anyway) that the judiciary would or should resolve such questions, but one that did concern both Hamilton and John Marshall. It is not surprising then that Marshall's court, disclaiming an authority to reconsider the legislature's judgment of the degree of necessity involved, would closely follow Hamilton's language, which, of course, would also prove more congenial to later, more positivistic courts: "If the end be clearly comprehended within any of the specified powers, and if the measure have an obvious relation to that end, and is not forbidden by any particular provision of the Constitution," Hamilton suggested, "it may safely be deemed to come within the compass of the national authority," especially if the measure proposed did not abridge "a preexisting right of any state or of any individual."[36]

In truth, however, none of these positions was without real dangers. Neither Hamilton nor Marshall every adequately answered Madison's essential questions, which, indeed, remain unanswered to this day. If "necessary" means no more than "needful, requisite, incidental, useful, or conducive to," as Hamilton maintained, what can possibly prevent a string of implications reaching any object whatever and gradually transforming a government of enumerated powers into a government with no practical limits at all (or limits defined only by exceptions such as those imposed by the Bill of Rights)?[37] And is it really possible, in any large and populous nation, for a single, unlimited government to be republican in character and spirit—"republican," that is, in something like the sense in which the great Virginians and many others of the founding generation defined that term? The great (and long) debate about the bank, accordingly, was only one more stage in the developing dispute about interpretation of the Constitution and the nature of the system it created.

A single chapter cannot follow every step in this dispute, but major issues and important landmarks can at least be mentioned. Thus, Madison's and Jefferson's alarm about the progress of "consolidation," their horror at the great degree to which the prophecies of Antifederalists appeared to be progressively unfolding, was ratcheted another notch by Hamilton's Report on Manufactures. Here again—and more decisively this time—the economic vision underlying the report was fundamentally at odds with the Virginians' different vision of the future. They would doubtless have opposed it on those grounds alone. But they were deeply troubled also by employment of the "general welfare" clause to justify the payment of bounties to encourage native manufactures. "The national legislature," Hamilton claimed,

> has express authority "to lay and collect taxes, duties, imposts and excises, to pay the debts and provide for the *common defense* and *general welfare*." . . . The power to *raise money* is *plenary* and *indefinite*; and the objects to which it may be *appropriated* are no less comprehensive than the payment of the public debts and the providing for the common defense and "*general welfare*." . . . The only qualifica-

tion of the generality of the phrase in question which seems to be admissible is this—that the object to which an appropriation of money is to be made be *general* and not *local*, its operation extending in fact, or by possibility, throughout the union, and not being confined to a particular spot.[38]

In previous debates about implicit powers, Madison explained to Henry Lee, even the greatest champions of broad construction had tied their arguments to the enumerated powers by way of the "necessary and proper" clause. "If not only the *means* but the *objects*" of the general government were rendered "unlimited" by appeal to the "general welfare" instead, "the parchment had better be thrown into the fire at once":

> It will no longer be a government possessing special powers taken from the general mass, but one possessing the general mass with special powers reserved out of it. And this change will take place in defiance of the true and universal construction and of the sense in which the instrument is known to have been proposed, advocated, and ratified.

"Everything, from the highest object of state legislation down to the most minute object of police would be thrown under the power of Congress," he told another correspondent, for almost any purpose "would admit the application of money and might be called, if Congress pleased, provisions for the general welfare."[39]

By this time, Madison was publicly (although anonymously) developing his fear of transmutation of the Constitution in several of his nineteen essays for the *National Gazette*, which he and Jefferson had helped found,[40] and Jefferson was saying much the same in conversations with the president, warning Washington that he had heard Hamilton say that the Constitution "was a shilly shally thing of mere milk and water, which could not last and was only good as a step to something better." Hamilton had sought in the Convention to "make an English constitution of it," and "all his measures" since were "tending to bring it to the same thing."[41]

Among the many reasons why these two Virginians feared a further concentration of authority in central hands, the necessary increase in executive responsibilities, a loosening of bonds of sympathy and intimate familiarity between the legislators and the people, and, in consequence, a loss of popular control of government were key. "Monarchy," or the gradual replacement of the current system with a British form of government, was shorthand for this bundle of concerns: a fear at once quite literal—that is, the distant outcome they envisioned if the current trends continued—and, for now, a way of saying briefly and dramatically how quickly, in their view, a replication of a British system of corrupting links between the secretary of the treasury and special-interest factions in the Congress, a Hamiltonian political economy, and Federalist interpretations of the Constitution were moving the new government toward "independence" from the people. This is why the two Virginians took such great alarm, again, at Hamilton's defense of Washington's authority to proclaim that the United States would pursue a "friendly and impartial" conduct during the war between Great Britain and the infant French Republic. The fundamental "heresy" that Jefferson urged Madison to cut apart before the public was not neutrality itself (though Madison did see the proclamation as entrenching on the legislature's clear authority to decide on war or peace) but Hamilton's construction of the scope of the executive prerogative in international relations. This, wrote Madison, was modeled on the practices and theory of monarchical Britain and "pregnant with inferences and consequences against which no ramparts in the Constitution could defend the public liberty, or scarcely the forms of republican government." If these doctrines were accepted, Madison warned the public,

> every power that can be deduced from them will be deduced and exercised sooner or later by those who may have an interest in so doing. . . . The history of government, in all its forms and in every period of time, ratified the danger. A people, therefore, who are so happy as to possess the inestimable blessing of a free and defined constitution cannot be too watchful against the introduction, nor too critical in tracing the consequences, of new principles and new constructions that may remove the landmarks of power.[42]

The argument about executive prerogative culminated, three years later, when Madison decided on a last-ditch stand against Jay's Treaty with Great Britain. Disastrous as Madison regarded this agreement, the Senate had conditionally approved it on June 24, 1795; Britain had accepted the conditions; and Washington proclaimed it in effect on February 29, 1796. Madison attempted to defeat it in the House of Representatives by refusing the appropriations necessary to fund the joint commissions it created. He acknowledged that the Constitution vested power over treaties in the president and Senate, but "taken literally and without limit," he maintained, this clearly clashed with the delegation to the whole Congress of powers to regulate commerce, declare war, raise armies, and such. In cases of this sort, he argued, the people's servants were obliged to construct the document in ways that "would best reconcile the several parts of the instrument with each other, and be most consistent with its general spirit and object." The Constitution surely did not mean to free the president and Senate, acting through the treaty power, to proceed without restraint on matters plainly entrusted only to Congress as a whole. On these grounds, he reasoned, treaties "required at the same time the legislative sanction and cooperation in those cases where the Constitution had given express and specific powers to the legislature." In such cases, certainly, the legislature would have to "exercise its authority with discretion," but it must still possess a will of its own.[43]

During these proceedings, Washington refused a House request to deliver papers relating to negotiation of the treaty and to Jay's instructions, partly on the grounds that a proposal at the Constitutional Convention to require that treaties be confirmed by laws had been specifically rejected by that body. Madison was forced into a further explanation of his basic principles of constitutional construction, for in his famous speech against the national bank, as some of his opponents gleefully remarked, he had himself recalled that the convention had specifically refused to enumerate a power to create corporations. But Madison was more embarrassed by the public clash with Washington than foes believed he ought to be by this apparent contradiction.[44] As he now explained, his reference to the convention in the speech of 1791 had been a passing comment, and the intent of the Constitutional Convention had never since been urged by anyone as a proper guide to the meaning of the Constitution.

Reexamination shows that Madison was right about his argument of 1791. Like the national bank, Jay's Treaty raised a question that had not, until that time, come clearly into view; and even Madison, as he repeatedly observed, could discover the implications of the Constitution only as new issues raised new questions. Constitutional interpretations had to be constructed over time, and no one's personal interpretation was unquestionably correct. But even in his argument against the bank, Madison had not depended mainly on the intentions of the Constitutional Convention. He had stood primarily on other ground: ground he had recurred to frequently in later writings and would take consistently from this point on. The Constitution, he had then suggested, was best understood as its friends and foes had understood it during the debates over its adoption. "In controverted cases, the meaning of the parties to the instrument"—the people who had ratified it through their several state conventions—was the most authoritative guide.

When the defenders of the Constitution were confronted with demands for amendments clarifying the reach of federal powers, Madison had said in 1791, they had replied that powers not confided to the federal government were retained by the states or the people "and that those given were not to be extended by remote implications." They had insisted that "the terms necessary and proper gave no additional powers." The explanatory declarations and proposed amendments offered by the state conventions were based on the same assumptions, and this general understanding had been confirmed by the Ninth and Tenth Amendments. "With all this evidence of the sense in which the Constitution was understood and adopted," it was both disgracefully dishonest and an outright usurpation to revert to an opposite construction to justify the bank.[45] "Whatever veneration might be entertained for the body of men who formed our Constitution," Madison added in 1796,

> the sense of that body could never be regarded as the oracular guide in expounding the Constitution. As the instrument came from them it was nothing more than the draft of a plan, nothing but a dead letter, until life and validity were breathed into it by the voice of the people, speaking through the several state conventions. If we were to look, therefore, for the meaning of the instrument, beyond the face of the instrument, we must look for it not in the general convention, which proposed, but in the state conventions, which accepted and ratified the Constitution.

Looking to this source—and beyond that, he might have added (as he had on earlier occasions), to the public writings on both sides of the ratification debate and to the amendments recommended by the several states—it was clear to him that the treaty power was a limited one. None of the state conventions had supposed that powers over commerce, war and peace, and even the disbursement of public funds could be assumed, in practice, by the Senate and executive alone.[46]

Madison's decision to retire from Congress may have been completed by his inability to hold his fellow Jeffersonian Republicans to a consistent strategy against Jay's Treaty. As all of them had feared, however, the agreement with Great Britain soon embroiled the nation in an argument with France. As John Adams replaced George Washington (and Jefferson became vice president), the trouble deepened into a limited naval war. And in the summer of 1798, the Federalists in Congress, over heated opposition, set about to use this crisis to repress their Republican opponents. French and Irish immigrants were mostly in that camp. Congress extended to fourteen years the residency required for naturalization and authorized the deportation of any alien whose presence seemed to the president a danger to the United States. Aliens and citizens alike were also subjected to a new sedition law that threatened with fines and imprisonment anyone who wrote, printed, uttered, or published "any false, scandalous and malicious writings against the government of the United States, or either house of the Congress of the United States, or the President of the United States, with intent to defame" them or to bring them "into contempt or disrepute." With these measures, the Republicans believed, the Federalist conspiracy against the Constitution—and against democracy itself—had burst into the open.

Enforced by a partisan judiciary, the crisis laws of 1798 imposed a bloodless reign of terror on the country. Under the Sedition Act or under color of a common law of seditious libel, all of the most important Republican newspapers in the country felt the sting of prosecutions, as did several opposition pamphleteers. The *Argus* and the *Time Piece*, the only Republican newspapers in New York City, were driven out of business. Benjamin Franklin Bache, whose Philadelphia *Aurora*

had replaced the *National Gazette* as the opposition's leading outlet, died while under indictment. But what could the defenders of the Constitution do when all three branches of the federal government united in a program that opponents saw not merely as a usurpation under cover of a forced interpretation of the fundamental law but also as a patent violation of express provisions of the Constitution— one that struck, moreover, at the very right that underpinned self-government itself? (In Congress, both Albert Gallatin and Edward Livingston had objected that the Sedition Act was a patent violation of the First Amendment and a potent threat to the people's underlying right to change their rulers through free elections, which depended on their freedom to express and circulate opinions.)

Jefferson's and Madison's response was to initiate or press the sort of protest that had greeted British measures early in the Revolution: much the sort of protest, ironically, that Hamilton, as well as Madison, appears to have envisioned back in 1788.[47] Each prepared a set of resolutions that they funneled to the legislatures of Kentucky and Virginia. Jefferson, as was his habit, was again the more extreme, but it was Madison's conception of the Constitution, introduced in *Federalist* 39, on which they both would build.

"The several states," Jefferson premised, had not united "on the principle of unlimited submission to their general government." Rather, by a "compact" to which each was party, "they constituted a general government for special purposes, delegated to that government certain definite powers," and reserved, "each state to itself, the residuary mass of right to their own self-government." Neither did they make this general government "the exclusive or final judge of the extent of the powers delegated to itself," for that would have made the general government's discretion, not the Constitution, "the measure of its powers." Instead, each state retained "an equal right to judge for itself, as well of infractions as of the mode and measure of redress." Act by act, his draft of the Kentucky Resolutions listed legislation in which Congress had assumed authority not delegated by the Constitution, mostly by construction but sometimes in the face of the explicit language of the Bill of Rights. Calling each of these examples "not law" but "altogether void and of no force," he argued that, in all such cases, "every state has a natural right . . . to nullify of their own authority all assumptions of power by others within their limits." Urging the other states to concur in similar declarations, he recommended also "measures of their own for providing that neither these acts nor any others of the general government not plainly and intentionally authorized by the Constitution shall be exercised within their respective territories."[48]

Kentucky's legislators deleted Jefferson's suggestion that the rightful remedy for federal usurpations was a nullification of such acts by each state acting on its own to prevent their operation within its respective bounds, calling only for the other states to unite in declarations that the federal acts were "void and of no force" and in "requesting their repeal." Madison was similarly cautious in his draft of resolutions for Virginia and would be on solid ground, years later, in insisting that he never said that any single state could constitutionally impede the operation of a federal law. Nevertheless, Virginia's legislature did "peremptorily declare," with Madison,

> that it views the powers of the federal government as resulting from the compact to which the states are parties; as limited by the plain sense and intention of the instrument constituting that compact; as no farther valid than they are authorised by the grants enumerated in that compact, and that in case of a deliberate, palpable, and dangerous exercise of powers not granted by the said compact, the states who are the parties thereto have the right, and are in duty bound, to interpose for arresting the progress of the evil, and for maintaining within their respective limits, the authorities, rights, and liberties appertaining to them.[49]

Like Jefferson, Madison attacked specific violations of amendments to the Constitution, together with the federal government's attempts

> to enlarge its powers by forced constructions of the constitutional charter . . . so as to destroy the meaning and effect of the particular enumeration which necessarily explains and limits the general phrases; and so as to consolidate the states by degrees into one sovereignty, the obvious tendency and inevitable consequence of which would be to transform the present republican system of the United States into an absolute, or at best a mixed monarchy.

Like Jefferson, Madison called on the states to concur not only in declaring these usurpations unconstitutional but also in declaring "that the necessary and proper measures will be taken by each for cooperating with this state in maintaining unimpaired the authorities, rights, and liberties reserved to the states respectively, or to the people."[50]

Madison would soon—and many times—regret his insufficient care in drafting the Virginia Resolutions. Though he had cautioned Jefferson against confusing the power of a state with that of its legislature,[51] he had not himself avoided language that confused the several senses in which "state" was commonly employed or language that could easily be taken, even if it was not meant, to recommend state actions to impede illegal measures "within their respective limits," which is pretty certainly what Jefferson appears to have envisioned and what South Carolina would attempt within the framer's lifetime. Seven other states responded to Virginia's and Kentucky's resolutions, all of them objecting, as New Hampshire did, "that the state legislatures are not the proper tribunals to determine the constitutionality of the laws of the general government" and several agreeing with Rhode Island that the Constitution "vests in the federal courts, exclusively, and in the Supreme Court . . . , ultimately, the authority" to make this judgment.[52] In 1799, Madison reentered the Virginia legislature to respond to these replies and clarify his stance (although without admitting that the language of the resolutions was his own).

But Madison did not retract the fundamental logic of Virginia's (or Kentucky's) interposition against the measures they protested. In *Federalist* 39, he had insisted that adoption of the Constitution was undoubtedly "a federal and not a national act," . . . "the act of the people as forming so many independent states, not as forming one aggregate nation." This, he had maintained, was obvious from the consideration that the Constitution was adopted neither by "the decision of a majority of the people of the union, nor from that of a majority of the states," but by the voluntary act of each of the states that approved it (each altering its own constitution in the process). Had the people been regarded "as forming one nation, the will of the majority of the whole people of the United States" would have bound the minority.[53] Now, in his Report of 1800, he reaffirmed that the Constitution was a federal compact whose parties were "the people composing" the several states "in their highest sovereign capacity." On these grounds, he still maintained "that where resort can be had to no tribunal superior to the authority of the parties, the parties themselves must be the rightful judges in the last resort, whether the bargain made has been pursued or violated." The federal courts were not such a superior tribunal since, on the opposite hypothesis, "the delegation of judicial power would annul the authority delegating it." In cases where there was "a deliberate, palpable and dangerous breach of the Constitution," cases "dangerous to the great purposes for which the Constitution was established," the parties to the compact could legitimately interpose "at least so far as to arrest the evil, to maintain their rights, and to preserve the Constitution." Otherwise, "there would be an end to all relief from usurped power . . . as well as a plain denial of the fundamental principle on which our independence itself was declared."[54]

Clause by clause, Madison elaborated and defended each of the resolutions of 1798. Federal usurpations by construction, he insisted, had begun as early as the law establishing the national bank. The sweeping clauses had been used repeatedly to justify assumptions of authority not clearly granted by the Constitution or intended by the parties to the compact. The Sedition Act and prosecutions under color of a federal common law of crimes were even worse. The former exercised a power "expressly and positively forbidden" by the First Amendment: a power "levelled against that right of freely examining public characters and measures, and of free communication thereon," which was essential to elective government itself. The latter claimed authority so broad as to completely overturn the concept of enumerated powers.[55]

In condemning the Sedition Act and other measures as transgressions of the Constitution, Virginia's general assembly, Madison insisted, was within its lawful bounds. If other states had joined it in such declarations, these and other protests by the people would have been sufficient to arrest the evils they condemned. Other means might also have been used, all undeniably permitted by the Constitution: petitions to the Congress, instructions to their senators to move amendments to the Constitution, or an exercise of the authority of three-fourths of the states to call a constitutional convention. If the Federalists of 1788 had thought it proper to support the Constitution by referring "to the intermediate existence of the state governments between the people and [the federal] government, to the vigilance with which they would descry the first symptoms of usurpation, and to the promptitude with which they would sound the alarm to the public," it was proper now for states to interpose against a train of measures that could wreck that

Constitution or extend the concentration of authority so far as to re-place elections by hereditary rule.[56]

Historically, it would seem hard to doubt that Madison was right about the way in which the Constitution had been made, and, histori-cally, although the other states refused to go along with the Virginia and Kentucky Resolutions, those resolutions did assist in furthering the protests that would help win the election of 1800 for men who were determined to retract the federal government into the limits they believed had been established by the people of the several states at its creation. The federal government *would* operate within enumerated limits long after the Civil War. But as the foremost framer of the Con-stitution lived to see, the compact theory held some dreadful dangers of its own. Its logic, in less subtle hands, marched readily to nullifica-tion and secession. For if, indeed, the people of the several states had been the parties to the federal compact, why are not these people (act-ing, it may be, through state conventions) the most authoritative judges of the things they had agreed to? Did they constitute a federal govern-ment that is itself, through its judiciary, final judge in its own cause?

Madison himself was nothing if not subtle, offering perhaps as good an answer to these questions as anyone has ever done. The Constitution was indeed, he would insist to both the nullifiers and their nationalist opponents, a compact entered into by the peoples of the several states, each covenanting with the others. Those peoples, ultimately sovereign, might have constituted a pure confederation. They might have framed a unitary national government. They chose, however, to do neither. In-stead, they each compacted with the others to create a system partly na-tional and partly federal in nature and "not to be explained so as to make it either."[57] They made themselves a single people *for the purposes enu-merated in that charter.* These facts, however, did not mean that any of these peoples, in their individual capacity, could constitutionally suspend the operation of a federal law, which was fully as authoritative, if the compact was created in this way, as if it had been entered into by "the people in their aggregate capacity, acting by a numerical majority of the whole."[58] No single party to the compact had a right to tell the others what the compact meant (or, presumably, to break the compact by a uni-lateral decision). Had the states retained an individual authority to judge the constitutionality of federal laws, the Constitution would have been a different document in different portions of the union. This trust was necessarily vested in the general government, acting through its own tribunals.[59] In case of usurpations by the general government, the states might make their declarations, might instruct their senators, might change their federal representatives through free elections, might call a constitutional convention, appealing to "the power that made the Constitution and can explain, amend, or remake it." Should all this fail, however, "and the power usurped be sustained in its oppressive exercise on a minority by a majority, the final course to be pursued by the minority must be a subject of calculation in which the degree of oppression, the means of resistance, the consequences of its failure, and consequences of its success must be the elements."[60] There is, that is to say, no constitutional right to nullify a federal law (or, presumably, to secede from the union). But there is always the right of revolution, exercise of which is likely to be greeted as revolutions usually are.[61]

This was not, of course, an unimpeachable solution to the riddle that had ruined the British Empire: how to keep the general government within the bounds defined by natural rights, by constitutional prescription, and by the powers vested in the other governments of a complex regime. It did not prevent secession. It begged the question, still, about exactly which dimensions of their lives the parties to the compact had intended to reserve from federal intrusions and what to do if most of the compacting parties proved to have a new or different understanding. In the long run, Madison's opponents at the founding may have been correct. Even if the people (or the peoples of the several states) are ultimately sovereign, *governmental* sovereignty may not in practice be divisible along a line that will not shift and can be recognized distinctly by an honest and dispassionate examination of the circumstances under which the compact has been made. No agency— not legislatures, federal courts, or even state conventions—can be universally acknowledged as a final judge of this division without encountering one problem or another. Europeans might take heed. Hard as it may be to forge a lasting and effective union, such a union, once established, may be even harder to confine. Certainly, America has never solved the federal puzzle.

NOTES

1. Thomas Jefferson to James Madison, December 16, 1786, in *The Republic of Letters: The Correspondence between Thomas Jefferson and James Madison,*

1776–1826, ed. James Morton Smith, 3 vols. paged consecutively (New York: Norton, 1995), 458.

2. The best recent discussion is Jack N. Rakove, *The Beginnings of National Politics: An Interpretive History of the Continental Congress* (Baltimore: Johns Hopkins University Press, 1991).

3. The classic study is Gordon S. Wood, *The Creation of the American Republic, 1776–1787* (Chapel Hill: University of North Carolina Press, 1969).

4. This paraphrases the language of *Federalist* 15, which had echoed throughout the Constitutional Convention. For the ease with which the convention agreed that repairs of the existing Articles of Confederation would not do, consider that the members needed less than three full days of direct comparison to reject the New Jersey alternative in favor of the amended Virginia Plan.

5. Virginia's ratification and proposed amendments, including a clause similar to New York's, can be found in *Creating the Bill of Rights: The Documentary Record from the First Federal Congress*, ed. Helen E. Veit, Kenneth R. Bowling, and Charlene Bangs Bickford (Baltimore: Johns Hopkins University Press, 1991), 17–21; New York's ratification is from Jonathan Elliot, ed., *The Debates in the Several State Conventions on the Adoption of the Federal Constitution* (New York: Burt Franklin, 1888), 1:327–31.

6. "Sweeping clauses" is a term of convenience (seldom used initially) for the opening and concluding clauses of Article I, section 8: "The Congress shall have power to lay and collect taxes, duties, imposts and excises, to pay the debts and provide for the common defense and general welfare of the United States" and "To make all laws which shall be necessary and proper for carrying into execution the foregoing powers, and all other powers vested by this Constitution in the government of the United States, or in any department or officer thereof."

7. *M'Culloch v. Maryland*, 1819, 4 Wheaton 316.

8. The quotations are from the Virginia Resolutions of 1798, in *The Papers of James Madison* (hereafter *PJM*), ed. William T. Hutchinson et al. (Chicago: University of Chicago Press, 1962–), 17:189–90.

9. Even Madison was far from perfectly consistent. In 1788 and 1789, he worried that the process of judicial review "makes the judiciary department paramount . . . to the legislature, which was never intended and can never be proper," anticipating Andrew Jackson ("Observations on Jefferson's Draft of a Constitution for Virginia," *PJM*, 11:293). In 1800, in defense of the Virginia Resolutions, he suggested that the courts *might* be the "last resort . . . in relation to the authorities of the other departments of the [general] government" but "not in relation to the rights of the parties to the constitutional compact," tempting John Calhoun (*PJM*, 17:424). Yet in the 1830s he insisted that the

nullifiers had gotten it all wrong, that the Supreme Court *was* the penultimate arbiter of disputes between the nation and the states, and that the nullifiers were dramatically at odds with the republican principle of majority control, a stand not wholly incompatible with that of Abraham Lincoln, who would settle the dispute by force. A full and superb discussion of Madison's late-life battle with the nullifiers is in Drew R. McCoy, *The Last of the Fathers: James Madison and the Republican Legacy* (Cambridge: Cambridge University Press, 1989), chap. 4.

10. As Madison told his father on July 5, 1789, the members were in "a wilderness without a single footstep to guide us," *PJM*, 12:278.

11. See his great speech of June 18, 1787, in *The Records of the Federal Convention of 1787*, ed. Max Farrand, rev. ed., 4 vols. (New Haven, Conn.: Yale University Press, 1937), 1:287.

12. See his preconvention letters to Edmund Randolph and George Washington, April 8 and 16, 1787, in *PJM*, 9:369, 383.

13. The crucial document here is an undated, private memorandum written shortly after the convention adjourned: "Conjectures about the New Constitution," in *The Papers of Alexander Hamilton* (hereafter *PAH*), ed. Harold C. Syrett and Jacob E. Cooke, 26 vols. (New York: Columbia University Press, 1961–1979), 4:275–77.

14. The quickest reference here may be his speech of June 29, 1787, in Farrand, *Records of the Convention*, 1:464–65.

15. See his letters to Jefferson of September 6, 1787, and October 24, 1787, *PJM*, 10:163–64, 207–16, suggesting that state equality in the Senate and the omission of a federal veto on state laws made it probable that the Constitution would "neither effectually answer its national object nor prevent the local mischiefs which everywhere excite disgusts against the state governments."

16. Madison to Edmund Randolph, October 21, 1787, *PJM*, 10:199 and note 4.

17. "Brutus," No. 1, in *The Documentary History of the Ratification of the Constitution*, ed. Merrill Jensen et al. (Madison: University of Wisconsin Press, 1976–), 1:412–21.

18. "Letters from the Federal Farmer," No. 7, in *The Anti-Federalist: An Abridgment, by Murray Dry, of the Complete Anti-Federalist Edited, with Commentary and Notes, by Herbert J. Storing* (Chicago: University of Chicago Press, 1985), 73–79.

19. *The Federalist*, ed. with intro. and notes by Jacob E. Cooke (Middleton, Conn.: Wesleyan University Press, 1961), no. 10, 63.

20. *Federalist* 51, 353.

21. This interlines and expands *Federalist* 51, 351.

22. For Madison's initial reservations and the reasons for his change of mind, see "Parchment Barriers and Fundamental Rights," in Lance Banning, *Jefferson and Madison: Three Conversations from the Founding* (Madison, Wis.: Madison House, 1995), 1–26.

23. *PJM*, 12:172–73.

24. Speech of June 17, 1789, *PJM*, 12:232–39.

25. Speech of June 17, 1789, *PJM*, 12:232–39. The long quotation is at 232, where Madison went on to argue that if such constitutional disputes could not be settled among the great departments themselves, "there is no resource left but the will of the community, to be collected in some mode to be provided by the Constitution or one dictated by the necessity of the case"— that is, the people, not one or another branch of the federal government, were the ultimate arbiters of constitutional disputes and could decide them by way of amendments or conventions.

26. "I feel great anxiety," he said (speech of June 17, 1789, *PJM*, 12: 232–39), when "called upon to give a decision . . . that may affect the fundamental principles of the government and liberty itself. But all that I can do is to weigh well everything advanced on both sides, with the purest desire to find out the true meaning of the Constitution and to be guided by that and an attachment to the true spirit of liberty."

27. Written constitutions, he would soon be writing, might justly "be pronounced the most triumphant epoch of [world] history," and it was critical that public opinion "should guarantee, with a holy zeal, these political scriptures from every attempt to add to or diminish from them." "Charters," *National Gazette*, January 18, 1792, reprinted in *PJM*, 14:192.

28. "Consolidation," *National Gazette*, December 3, 1791, reprinted in *PJM*, 14:139.

29. "Government of the United States," *National Gazette*, February 4, 1792, reprinted in *PJM*, 14:218.

30. Speech of February 2, 1791, reprinted in *PJM*, 14:372–82.

31. Stuart Leibiger, *Founding Friendship: George Washington, James Madison, and the Creation of the American Republic* (Charlottesville: University Press of Virginia, 1999), is a very recent study.

32. *The Papers of Thomas Jefferson*, ed. Julian P. Boyd et al. (Princeton, N.J.: Princeton University Press, 1950–), 19:275–80.

33. *PAH*, 8:62–134.

34. Although, as fierce as he had been in his denunciation of the bank, Jefferson had ended his opinion by advising the president (consistently with his republican principles) that he should defer to the legislature's judgment if he remained uncertain of the constitutionality of a measure.

35. *Federalist* 44, 303–4, including, "It would be easy to show if it were necessary that no important power delegated by the Articles of Confederation has been or can be executed by Congress without recurring more or less to the doctrine of *construction* or *implication*. As the powers delegated under the new system are more extensive, the government . . . would find itself still more distressed with the alternative of betraying the public interest by doing nothing or of violating the Constitution by exercising powers indispensably necessary and proper, but at the same time not *expressly* granted."

36. Compare the language of *M'Culloch v. Maryland*, "Let the end be legitimate, let it be within the scope of the constitution, and all means which are appropriate, which are plainly adapted to that end, which are not prohibited, but consist with the letter and spirit of the constitution, are constitutional."

37. Which was just what Madison complained of in the aftermath of the court's decision on the bank, sounding almost like a critic of twentieth-century uses of the commerce clause: The problem with *M'Culloch* was "the high sanction given to [excessive] latitude in expounding the Constitution. . . . In the great system of political economy, having for its general object the national welfare, everything is related immediately or remotely to every other thing; and consequently a power over any one thing, if not limited by some obvious and precise affinity, may amount to a power over every other." A rule of construction "as broad and as pliant" as Marshall's would have defeated the ratification of the Constitution, Madison insisted. "It has been the misfortune, if not the reproach, of other nations that their governments have not been freely and deliberately established by themselves. It is the boast of ours that such has been its source and that it can be altered by the same authority only which established it. . . . It is anxiously to be wished, therefore, that no innovations may take place in other modes, one of which would be a constructive assumption of powers never meant to be granted. If the powers be deficient, the legitimate source of additional ones is always open, and ought to be resorted to." Madison to Spencer Roane, September 2, 1819, in *The Mind of the Founder: Sources of the Political Thought of James Madison*, ed. Marvin Meyers, rev. ed. (Hanover, N.H.: University Press of New England, 1981), 359–62.

38. *PAH*, 10:302–3.

39. Madison to Henry Lee and Madison to Edmund Pendleton, January 11, 8, and 21, 1792, in *PJM*, 14:180, 193–96, 220–24.

40. The *National Gazette* essay "Charters" appeared concurrently with the letters to Pendleton and Lee.

41. See his remarks on the "general welfare" clause in his report of a conversation of February 29, 1792, in *Thomas Jefferson: Writings*, ed. Merrill D.

Peterson (New York: Literary Classics of the U.S., 1984), 677, and the report of a conversation of October 1, 1792, therein, 682.

42. "Letters of Helvidius," numbers 2 and 4, replying to Hamilton's "Letters of Pacificus," *PJM*, 14:80, 106–7.

43. Speech of March 10, 1796, *PJM*, 17:255–63. Obviously, this was hardly "strict construction," but it has been my point throughout that "strict construction" is a crude characterization of Madison's way of interpreting the charter.

44. Perhaps he should have been embarrassed, too, that he had really misremembered or offered a challengeable interpretation of the episode he had in mind. Benjamin Franklin had suggested the addition to the enumerated powers of one to cut canals, and Madison himself had proposed extending this to a power to create corporations. These propositions were indeed rejected, but, as Hamilton noted in his opinion on the bank, this happened after a debate in which some members had objected that the power would permit a bank, but others seemed to think that a power to create corporations was already implicit.

45. *PJM*, 13:374, 380–81. And, certainly, both Madison and Hamilton had insisted that opponents need not fear the "sweeping clauses." See Hamilton's *Federalist* 33, 204–7, and Madison's *Federalist* 41 and 44, 277–78, 302–6.

46. Speech of April 6, 1796, *PJM*, 17:290–301, quotations at 294–96. The fullest discussion of this congressional debate, emphasizing how it moved discussion of the constructions of the Constitution toward an insistence on considering the records of the state conventions and the dialogue between Federalists (especially "Publius") and Antifederalists, is in Saul Cornell, *The Other Founders: Anti-Federalism and the Dissenting Tradition in America, 1788–1828* (Chapel Hill: University of North Carolina Press, 1999), 221–30.

47. Every federal usurpation, said Madison's *Federalist* 44 (on the "necessary and proper" clause) would be an invasion of the rights of the states; "these will be ever ready to mark the innovation, to sound the alarm to the people, and to exert their local influence in effecting a change of federal representatives" (305). Every state government, he added (*Federalist* 46, 320), "would espouse the common cause. A correspondence would be opened. Plans of resistance would be concerted. . . . The same combination in short would result from an apprehension of the federal as was produced by the dread of a foreign yoke; and unless the projected innovation should be voluntarily renounced, the same appeal to a trial of force would be made in the one case as was made in the other." "The state governments," Hamilton concurred (*Federalist* 28, 179–80), "will in all possible contingencies afford complete security against invasions of the public liberty by the national authority." "Possessing all the organs of civil power and the confidence of the people, they can at once adopt

a regular plan of opposition, in which they can combine all the resources of the community. They can readily communicate with each other in the different states and unite their common force for the protection of their common liberty." The state legislatures, he had already said, would "constantly have their attention awake to the conduct of the national rulers and will be ready enough, if anything improper appears, to sound the alarm to the people and not only to be the voice but if necessary the arm of their discontent" (*Federalist* 26, 169).

48. Jefferson's rough draft and fair copy of the resolutions are printed side by side, together with the resolutions as actually adopted, in *The Works of Thomas Jefferson*, ed. Paul Leicester Ford, 12 vols. (New York: G. P. Putnam's Sons, 1904), 8:458–79.

49. *PJM*, 17:189.

50. *PJM*, 17:189–90.

51. Madison to Jefferson, December 29, 1798, *PJM*, 17:191–92: "On the supposition that the [state] is clearly the ultimate judge of infractions, it does not follow that the [legislature] is the legitimate organ, especially as a convention was the organ by which the compact was made. This was a reason of great weight for using general expressions that would leave to other states a choice of the modes possible of concurring" with Virginia's views. (But, of course, as South Carolina, followed later by its southern sisters, was to prove, it would be easy enough to constitute a convention rather than the legislature as an organ.)

52. Henry Steele Commager, ed., *Documents of American History* (Englewood Cliffs, N.J.: Prentice Hall, 1988), 1:184–85.

53. *Federalist* 39, 254.

54. *PJM*, 17:307–51, quotations at 309–11.

55. *PJM*, 17:307–51, quotations at 317.

56. *PJM*, 17:307–51, quotations at 350.

57. "Notes on Nullification (1835–36)," in Meyers, *The Mind of the Founder*, 437. Both simpler forms had proven incompatible with "individual rights, public order, [or] external safety," Madison added, and those who would insist on making the Constitution one or the other "aim[ed] a deadly blow at the last hope of true liberty on the face of the earth" ("Notes on Nullification," 441).

58. "Notes on Nullification," 440.

59. Madison to Spencer Roane, June 29, 1821, in "Notes on Nullification," 368.

60. "Notes on Nullification," 434.

61. The issues raised by the Sedition Act and by the long succession of federal "abuses" in the years since 1791 were very like the ones James Otis and

other revolutionary pamphleteers had struggled with from 1764 until the Declaration of Independence. Like Otis, Jefferson, and even John Locke, Madison insisted in the Resolutions of 1798 and in the Report of 1800 that only a long succession of tyrannical abuses could justify resistance. But such a long succession of abuses was exactly what the revolutionaries, the Jeffersonian Republicans, and the secessionists of 1861 believed that they were faced with— and exactly what Parliament, the Federalists, and the general government of 1861 denied were unconstitutional at all.

• 3 •

The Gentry and the People

𝒯he great debate about a sound interpretation of the infant federal Constitution was itself, when we have probed it to its bottom, a dispute about the nature of a sound relationship in a republic between the rulers and the ruled. Confronted with the plan for federal reform, thoughtful Antifederalists advanced a multitude of sharp objections, sometimes from conflicting regional perspectives. If anything united them, however, in addition to their universal fear that fundamental rights were not secured, it was their worry that the plan would lead inexorably to a progressive concentration of authority in central hands and that a unitary national government could not, in practice, be a genuine republic. "I never heard of two supreme coordinate powers in one and the same country," a Virginia Antifederalist complained. "I cannot conceive how it can happen." Sooner or later, a colleague agreed, all power would be sucked into the mighty vortex of the federal government. And no one, said a third, could think that a single national government could "suit so extensive a country, embracing so many climates, and containing inhabitants so very different in manners, habits, and customs." Sixty-five representatives—the number planned for the first lower house—could not "know the situation and circumstances of all the inhabitants of this immense continent." But "representatives ought to ... mix with the people, think as they think, feel as they feel— ought to be ... thoroughly acquainted with their interest and condition." If this were not the case, the government would not be really representative at all.[1]

The most important current scholar of the founding sides with these opponents of reform. "The Constitution was intrinsically an aristocratic document designed to check the democratic tendencies of the period," writes Gordon S. Wood. Federalists supported it for the same reasons that Antifederalists opposed it: because it would forbid the sort of populistic measures many states had taken in response to current economic troubles; because it would deliver power to a "better sort" of people; "because its very structure and detachment from the people would work to exclude those who were not rich, well born, or prominent from exercising political power."[2] The Revolution, Wood remarks, had democratized the nation's politics and loosed a radical contagion. After 1776, the lower houses in the states, larger and more frequently elected than the old colonial assemblies, were filled with men whose social stature would have kept them out of such positions during the colonial years. Fundamentally unchecked by poorly balanced constitutions, many of these lower houses answered popular appeals for some relief from postwar economic troubles by supporting paper money, moratoriums on taxes, and other measures that endangered property or rendered the new governments unable to fulfil their obligations. Thus, the members of the Constitutional Convention overwhelmingly agreed with Elbridge Gerry that the nation suffered from "an excess of democracy" and yearned for restoration of an ordered liberty before the system spun completely out of gentlemen's control.[3]

But Wood is only partly right about the friends of federal reform, and he is only partly right because his scholarship has always underestimated two important facts about the making of the Constitution. In the first place, few political responsibilities, apart from regulation of the nation's commerce, were actually shifted into federal hands by the adoption of the Constitution. In theory, even the powers to borrow money, raise an army, and assess taxation were already vested in the federal government by the Articles of Confederation. From this perspective, friends of the reform were right to say that the Constitution proposed "much less . . . the addition of NEW POWERS to the Union than . . . the invigoration of its ORIGINAL POWERS"; that, for the most part, it only "substitute[d] a more effectual mode of administering" the powers that had long ago been trusted to a general Congress— indeed, to a single-chamber government *no* part of which was chosen directly by the people.[4] The Constitutional Convention quite deliberately created not a unitary great republic but rather a system only partly national in nature—a system, too, that was deliberately intended to be grounded more directly on the people than the old one was. And hardly any of its members thought it should have gone significantly further toward consolidated central power.[5]

In the second place, which is the place to which this brings us, the proponents of the Constitution were by no means unified in how they hoped a stronger central government would work or in their hopes about the work that it would do. Alexander Hamilton, as we have seen, did hope to shift authority increasingly to central hands and federal authority to branches least immediately responsive to the people.[6] During the convention, in a speech that tied his tail to cans that clattered through the rest of his career, he candidly admitted that his faith in governments deriving wholly from elections had been gravely shaken since the early Revolution, that he doubted now that any government without hereditary parts could ever prove consistent with security for private rights or with a requisite consistency and vigor. But even Hamilton had not abandoned hope. Here and elsewhere he insisted that a number of expedients could still be tried before abandoning the revolutionary dream. He did, however, urge the great convention to move as far as democratic sentiment would possibly permit toward the incorporation in the Constitution of a "permanent will" distinct from the will of the democratic many, favoring an upper house and an executive holding office during good behavior and approaching the "independence" of the British king and lords as closely as elective principles allowed.[7]

But there were other framers, led by Hamilton's collaborator in the classic exegesis of the Constitution, who were fully as determined as the young New Yorker to construct additional securities for fundamental rights, who quite agreed that lower houses in the states were *so* responsive to the whims of the majority that private rights and public good were both endangered, but who thoroughly condemned the thought that liberty should be protected by "creating a will in the community independent of the majority,"[8] men for whom, as for their Antifederalist opponents, it was not sufficient to define a genuine republic as any government derived entirely from direct or indirect elections.[9] In *Federalist* 10, his first in the extended series, Madison insisted that the plan for constitutional reform was perfectly consistent with "the spirit" as well as with the form "of popular government," and, when he opened his uninterrupted string of contributions to the classic, he admitted that the Constitution's advocates "must abandon it as no longer defensible" if it could not be shown to be "strictly republican" in "aspect" as well as in "form."[10] Nothing occupied this framer more intently through the corpus of his numbers than the need to answer Antifederalist complaints that even the House of Representatives was hardly democratic to begin with and that, as power gravitated more completely into central hands, the system would eventually result in total loss of popular control.

Madison, with many other Federalists, did hope that the enlarged election districts of the great republic would favor the selection of a better class of rulers: representatives who would be less inclined to sacrifice the rights of the minority or the enduring public good to "temporary or partial considerations."[11] But the great Virginian neither wanted nor expected representatives who would not re-present the character and interests of their constituencies.[12] He admitted that the Antifederalists were right to warn that federal representatives could not be as familiar "with all [the people's] local circumstances and lesser interests" as the hundreds of more ordinary men who represented them in lower houses in the states.[13] For just this reason, he insisted, federal representatives were not to act on matters that required an intimate familiarity with local situations.[14] "The powers of the federal government are enumerated," he insisted; "it can only operate in certain cases."[15] For these cases, the House of Representatives *was* large enough "for the purposes of safety, of local information, and of diffusive sympathy with the whole society."[16] On these matters, federal representatives *could* be trusted to reflect the voters' interests, character, and will. They were to be elected by the body of the people: by everyone who had the right to vote in state elections. Every rational precaution for maintaining their dependence on the people had been taken. Representatives would enter on their offices with gratitude toward voters. They could make no law that would not be as binding on themselves, their families, and their connections as on everyone else. And they would be compelled to face another poll in just two years.[17] As long as this was so, the Constitution would not break the democratic bond between the rulers and the ruled: the "communion of interests and sympathy of sentiments" that joins the legislators to the people.[18] And it was most unlikely that the House of Representatives would be unable to defend its powers from encroachments by the other branches.[19]

Madison was conscious, as he framed and justified the Constitution, that the public trust could be betrayed in two ways, not just one: by a majority pursuing factious ends or by ambitious legislators who escaped a due dependence on the people and pursued a partial interest of their own.[20] Privately, he even noted that the same conditions that would make it hard for a tyrannical majority to form in an enlarged republic might also make it hard to forge "a defensive concert . . . against the oppression of those entrusted with the administration."[21] In 1788, of course, the need for such a concert hardly ranked among his salient concerns. In the midst of this enormous national debate and in the aftermath of Shays's Rebellion and the bitter arguments about responses to the postwar slump, no one had much cause to fear that a quiescent public would endanger the United States.[22] Accordingly, in *Federalist* 10, the framer barely glanced at the possibility that minorities might pose a danger: "If a faction consists of less than a majority," he wrote, "relief is supplied by the republican principle, which enables the majority to defeat its sinister views by regular vote."[23]

By 1791, however, circumstances had completely changed—at least in Madison's and Jefferson's opinions—and, at this point, the two Virginians set about in earnest to address the problem of excessive disconnection of the legislators from the people. In doing so, with Hamilton's unwitting help, they did as much as any figures of the age to popularize the system, and this ought to draw attention to an interesting point. Adoption of the Constitution did not check, much less reverse, the ever-swelling tide of popular involvement that had started early in the Revolution and would shape the nation's politics for years to come. Just the opposite was clearly and inevitably the case. By giving ordinary voters, for the first time, an essential part in choosing national officials and debating national needs, the Constitution guaranteed a wider popular involvement in a broader range of public choices and issues.[24] Moreover, studies that portray this process as a rising of the people over uniform resistance by an anxious gentry miss a critical dimension of the story. *Some* gentlemen resisted it as long as they were able. Nearly all would have preferred an outcome less completely democratic than they got. None of them envisioned a republic even distantly fulfilling modern democratic wishes: multiracial, multicultural, and with equality between the sexes. But in the 1790s, as early in the Revolution, arguments *among* the gentry were absolutely fundamental to the rising of the people, and democracy advanced as quickly as it did because there was a segment of the national elite who were determined that it should.

By the spring of 1791, when Washington approved the national bank, Madison's and Jefferson's concern about the infant government's directions was sharpening into outright alarm. Two years before, during the deliberations on the tariff—and only twenty days after the First Federal Congress convened—Madison had blasted the New Englanders' unwillingness to shoulder their fair share of national taxation.[25] Over the succeeding years, through arguments about the seat of government and the assumption of state debts, the eastward tilt of national policies seemed ever more apparent to his mind. Measure after measure seemed to favor the New England states and the commercial and financial interests. The federal balance seemed to tip increasingly toward greater central power. Madison was thrice defeated in his effort to discriminate against the British in retaliation for their navigation laws. With the creation of the bank, the general shape of Hamilton's design to imitate the British system of finance became a good deal clearer in his mind, and Madison was more and more convinced that imitation of the modern system of finance was imitation also of the British system of administration, characterized by a corrupting link between the treasury and grasping and dependent members of the Congress.[26] The twisting of the Constitution into something that had never been adopted by the people was another potent worry. Through nearly all of it, however, there was little protest "out of doors," beyond the walls of Congress.[27]

Even worse, as Thomas Jefferson conceived it, there was little but enthusiastic celebration of the new administration in the single newspaper with any claim to national circulation—that and the "Discourses on Davila," which were yet another reason for concern. Like Madison, with whom he talked at every turn, Jefferson had grown increasingly uncomfortable with the direction of affairs, peppering his correspondence with inquiries as to how these policies were "relished" in the country at large.[28] More than Madison, perhaps, he was increasingly disturbed as well by the tenor of conversations in the higher social circles in the city. Surprising numbers of the Philadelphia elite were more and more alarmed about developments in France, fearful that commotions there would reignite the radical contagion in the new United States, vocal in their praise of British institutions, and contemptuous of rising popular involvement in political affairs. The *Gazette of the United States*, he told his son-in-law, was "a paper of pure Toryism, disseminating the doctrine of monarchy, aristocracy, and the exclusion of the influence of the people."[29] "Davila," which was obviously penned by Vice President John Adams and had been running in that paper over the preceding months, was an obvious example, a series nothing short of counterrevolutionary in its content and intent. Thus, three days after Washington approved the national bank, Jefferson invited Philip Freneau to take a part-time place as translator in the Department of State, assuring him that the responsibilities would be so light that they should not impede another calling, obviously hoping that the editor and poet, a friend of Madison's since college, would come to Philadelphia and start a paper that would counter the "Tory" sheet. And before the two Virginians could persuade Freneau to seat his semiweekly in Philadelphia instead of in New Jersey, Jefferson had inadvertently initiated a campaign to rouse the public, a campaign in which the *National Gazette* would be the major organ.[30]

Part 1 of Thomas Paine's *The Rights of Man* was published in London in March 1791, not long before the adjournment of the First Federal Congress. Madison obtained a copy and passed it on to Jefferson before departing for New York to press Freneau and to enjoy the interlude between congressional sessions. Jefferson sent it on, as he had been instructed, together with a little note remarking that he was "extremely pleased to find . . . that something is at length to be publicly said against the heresies which have sprung up among us," having little doubt that Americans would rally again around Paine's defense of Lockean contractualism, republican government, and written constitutions against the challenge of Edmund Burke's *Reflections on the Revolution in France*. In this way the pamphlet reached a printer, who issued an American edition on May 3 with a preface quoting the secretary of state.[31]

Jefferson was mortified to see his note in print, aimed as it could only be at Adams. Hamilton, with whom he had struggling in the cabinet, was "open-mouthed" against him, he complained, saying that his comments marked an "opposition to the government" and trying, thus, to turn back on Jefferson himself the "censures I meant for the [real] enemies of the government, to wit those who want to change it into a monarchy." His ancient friendship with John Adams was endangered. Within a month, his little note would loose a national furor.

To Adams, certainly, the treatise on Davila could not have been more roundly misconstrued. To him, the series was another volley in the cannonade that he had fired at French philosophers in 1787 in the three fat volumes of his *Defence of the Constitutions of Government of the United States*. In all these works, it was precisely "heresy"—French support for unicameral regimes—that Adams understood himself as trying to combat. The nation's second magistrate was one of its most famous spokesmen for a neoclassical defense of balanced governments in which the many and the few would each control one legislative house and would be refereed and balanced by a single, strong executive who must be independent of them both. Horrified by what he saw as French contempt for the universal lessons of history, convinced that concentration of authority in a single legislative house could only concentrate all power in an irresponsible few, and worried that the radical ideas of Condorcet, Turgot, and their admirers might infect the new United States, he mounted an impassioned, deeply learned argument for the superiority of balanced constitutions.

The more he wrote, however, the more John Adams managed to provoke increasing puzzlement and anger—even in the most astute among his readers. He seemed to them not merely to prefer the British constitution to the unicameral experiment now under way in France but even to commend the British mixed regime as better than any government derived entirely from elections. His adherence to a theory that assimilated the American and British constitutions was repulsive to republicans who thought that the United States had made a world-historical departure from their British roots. Adams, even Madison suggested, hardly had a solid reason to complain about Jefferson's note. "Under a mock defense of the republican constitutions of this country, he attacked them with all the force he possessed, and this in a book with his name to it whilst he was a representative of his country" in England. Even as vice president, Madison believed, Adams had "constantly been at work in the same cause. . . . Surely if it be innocent and decent in one servant of the public thus to write attacks against its government, it cannot be very criminal or indecent in another to patronize a written defense of the principles on which that government is founded."[32]

Through the spring and into the fall of 1791, between the adjournment of the First Congress and the meeting of the Second, the controversy started by "Davila" and by Jefferson's note on Paine spread rapidly throughout the country, drawing growing numbers into national disputes. On June 8, the (Boston) *Columbian Centinel* published the first of eleven letters by "Publicola," which everyone thought was Adams's rejoinder to Jefferson and Paine, though they were actually written by his son, John Quincy.[33] Dozens of responses to "Publicola" appeared in newspapers throughout the country, condemning the vice president's supposed apostasy from republican principles and often saying publicly what Jefferson was saying in private: that the Federalists intended to reintroduce hereditary rule.[34] By October 31, the ground was well prepared for the initial issue of the *National Gazette*, in which a host of anonymous writers, led by Madison and by Freneau himself, would rapidly develop a coherent ideology condemning nearly every measure since the funding of the debt as part of an elaborate conspiracy to undermine the Constitution and prepare the way for the subversion of the federal republic.

If arguments about the funding of the debt, a national bank, or tariff policies had been too recondite to stir the body of the people, arguments about the threat of aristocracy and monarchy were not. The most distinctive feature of the rising popular assertiveness that was to mark the early years of the republic was undoubtedly the fierce resentment of so many ordinary people of the condescension or contempt so evident among so many of the national elite.

Madison himself wrote nineteen essays for the *National Gazette*, several of them on the perils of consolidation and the character of sound relationships between the people and their rulers.[35] Four years before, he had insisted that a free regime would have to find a middle ground between excessive concentration of authority in distant, unresponsive rulers and power *so* responsive to the whims of state majorities that neither private rights nor long-term public needs would be secure. At that time, he was convinced that such a mean had actually been struck in the new Constitution. Whatever "theoretic politicians" said, his numbers of *The Federalist* insisted, governmental sovereignty *could* be successfully and lastingly divided in a system where both the state and federal governments were to be "substantially dependent" on the people, creatures of a common master who would guard the constitutional division of responsibilities and ultimately guide them both. By 1791, however, the people seemed disturbingly complacent in the face of tendencies and programs that he now believed might be deliberately counterrevolutionary in intent. The federal government was not responding to the agricultural majority of people. The advantages—and vulnerabilities—of large, compound republics would have to be rethought. The people's role and the conditions necessary if they were to play that role would have to be considered more intensively than he had earlier believed.

As critical for guarding liberty as institutional checks might be, Madison now wrote, the constitutional division of authority between the state and general governments, together with the checks and balances in each, were "neither the sole nor the chief palladium of constitutional liberty." Their operation was not automatic. It depended, in the end, on the voters. "The people, who are the authors of this blessing, must also be its guardians. Their eyes must be ever ready to mark, their voice to pronounce, and their arm to repel or repair aggressions on the authority of their constitutions."[36]

"Public opinion sets bounds to every government, and is the real sovereign in every free one," Madison now suggested.[37] But in a large, complex, diverse republic where the tiny general government touched lightly on the lives of ordinary people who often lacked the information necessary to remain abreast of federal decisions, it could be difficult for a majority to coalesce, to find its voice, and to enforce its will. "The larger a country, the less easy for its real opinion to be ascertained, and the less difficult [for it] to be counterfeited" or mistaken. The larger the country, moreover, the more effective public opinion would prove, once this opinion was determined or even "presumed." "The more extensive a country, the more insignificant is each individual in his own eyes," the greater therefore is the need for "local organs" of opinion, and the greater is the danger that the difficulty of combining with effect may lead to "universal silence" and indifference in the people, freeing their rulers to follow a "self-directed course."[38]

National majorities, in other words, do not appear by magic, by some process of spontaneous combustion in the population. "Good roads, domestic commerce, a free press, and particularly a *circulation of newspapers through the entire body of the people* and *representatives going from and returning among every part of them"* were critical if genuine opinion was to form, the people were to play their proper role, and liberty was to be secure.[39] Opponents might believe that "the people are stupid, suspicious, licentious," that "they should think of nothing but obedience, leaving the care of their liberties to their wiser rulers." Republicans, by contrast, knew that, though "the people may betray themselves," it does not follow that they should surrender, blindfold, "to those who have an interest in betraying them. Rather, conclude that the people ought to be enlightened, to be awakened, to be united, that after establishing a government they should watch over it, as well as obey it." An enlightened people, in the end, were not only the best keepers of their liberty, they were the only keepers with whom liberty was safe.[40]

The *National Gazette*, soon joined by other broadsheets that reprinted many of its essays and contributed a number of their own, accomplished some of what the two Virginia gentlemen intended. Hamilton was so alarmed about the rising public criticism of his programs that he launched a public counterblow against his rivals by attacking Jefferson's connection with Freneau.[41] Jefferson's defenders, led by Madison and James Monroe, sprang quickly to their friend's defense.[42] Through the summer and into the fall of 1792, as the controversy that started at the seat of government rippled out through newspapers across the country, the public everywhere was caught up in the spectacle of public war between the greatest ministers of state. Hundreds of ordinary citizens, many of whom had had slight interest in national issues (and no direct role in national politics until the Constitution was adopted), were mobilized by this dispute.

But how was their opinion to be formulated, ascertained, and properly asserted? Public demonstrations were a channel, and these became more numerous and rowdy in the spring of 1793 as an ambassador arrived from revolutionary France, Washington proclaimed neutrality, and Madison and Hamilton wrote one another to a standstill in an argument about the reach of the executive's prerogative in international relations. Toasts, petitions, and addresses at such meetings, printed in the papers and occasionally reprinted far and wide, were yet another vehicle for popular opinion. As Hamilton moved increasingly behind neutrality, however, Madison became increasingly concerned about the "counterfeiting" of opinion. While his essays of "Helvidius" were still in process, he complained to Jefferson about "the language of the towns" and misinterpretations of the people's feelings likely to be fostered by resolutions such as those adopted by a Richmond meeting on August 17. "The Anglican Party," he charged, was using these to lead the people "from their honorable connection with [France] into the arms and ultimately into the government of G[reat] B[ritain]." To counteract them, he explained, he and James Monroe had drafted model resolutions to be circulated through the counties in Virginia, where "the real sentiments of the people"—"the agricultural, which is the commanding part of the society"—could be collected by their leaders.[43] County meetings might expose the counterfeiting of the people's sentiments in resolutions coming from the cities. But county meetings and their resolutions would not grow without some tending of the grass. Unless the people's local leaders organized and guided such assemblies, the country people would be uninformed and "too inert" to speak.[44]

Welcome also to the champions of popular alertness and involvement were the popular societies that burst into activity throughout the country in the spring of 1793, nearly all of them as vigilant against "aristocrats" at home as in supporting France against the European coalition.[45] Gentlemen like Madison or Jefferson were hardly democrats by modern standards. The public opinion that Madison hoped would rule was undoubtedly the well-considered reason of the people, not their unconsidered, unenlightened, or spontaneous first impulse. Like Jefferson, who used this term while he did not, Madison unquestionably believed that "natural aristocrats" should govern, and he was not naive enough to think that popular opinion would emerge without its shapers, that resolutions and addresses would be written by assemblages of people on their own. But "natural aristocracy," the two Virginians did believe, should rest exclusively on merit and the people's recognition, not on wealth or birth or other "accidental" reasons for distinction (which is why they took such issue with John Adams).[46] And the natural aristocrats who led and shaped opinion should never cease attending to the people's needs and voice, which helps explain why Madison, despite his veneration for the great commander, risked a public confrontation with the president himself when Washington condemned the popular societies in his annual message of 1794.

Throughout his first administration, Washington had managed to remain above the clamors and suspicions rising all around him. In the end, however, Washington himself was very much a friend of public order and could not dissociate himself from the indictments of administration policies by "that rascal Freneau," by other scribblers in the press, and by "certain self-created societies" whose denunciations of the excise tax and running war with the domestic "aristocracy" he blamed for the Whiskey Rebellion in western Pennsylvania during the summer of 1794.[47]

Though Madison and Jefferson had watched uneasily as 13,000 federalized militia, with Hamilton along to stand in for the absent secretary of war, had marched across the mountains to suppress the Whiskey Rebellion, both of them condemned the Pennsylvanians' conduct. The "real authors" of the rebellion, Madison told James Monroe, "were, in the most effectual manner, doing the business of despotism":

> You well know the general tendency of insurrections to increase the momentum of power. You will recollect the particular effect of what happened some years ago in Massachusetts. Precisely the same calamity [for republicanism] was to be dreaded on a larger scale in this case. There were enough, as you may well suppose, ready to give the same turn to the crisis and to propagate the same impressions from it. It happened most auspiciously, however, that with a spirit truly republican, the people everywhere and of every description condemned the resistance to the will of the majority and obeyed with alacrity the call to vindicate the laws.[48]

Nevertheless, when Federalists in Congress sought to echo Washington's denunciation of the clubs, Madison, who privately described the president's address as the greatest mistake of his political career, mounted a determined opposition.[49] The publications and opinions of the popular societies, he told the House of Representatives, could not be censured by the legislative body. "Opinions are not the objects of legislation. . . . If we advert to the nature of republican government, we shall find that the censorial power is in the people over the government, and not in the government over the people."[50] Privately, indeed, his feelings were even stronger. He thought it "indefensible in reason" and "dangerous in practice" to accept the principles that "arbitrary denunciations may punish what the law permits and what the legislature has no right, by law, to prohibit," that "the government may stifle all censures whatever on its misdoings; for if it be itself the judge, it will never allow any censures to be just, and if it can suppress censures flowing from one lawful source, it may [also suppress] those flowing from any other—from the press and from individuals as well as from societies, etc."[51]

But there were serious—and perfectly republican—positions on both sides of this issue. From their first appearance, democratic clubs had met with a resistance that was not as ill-considered, antidemocratic, or unthinking as it may appear to modern sensibilities and tastes.[52] Popular opinion, after all, may well be "counterfeited" in a wide variety of ways, and noninclusive, extralegal "pressure groups" (as we might call them), constituted as so many standing watchdogs on the people's legal representatives and measures, were by definition factions, easily and not unjustifiably perceived as standing challenges to real majority control. "Do the people require intermediary guides betwixt them and the constituted authorities?" asked a writer in the *New York Daily Gazette*. "Are they chosen by the people?"[53] These clubs, another writer said,

> are as unfounded and unknown to our constitution and laws as were the Cincinnati, and the object of their institution and the views and principles of their leaders are much more alarming and dangerous to society. The former were chargeable only with a foolish pride for an empty distinction, at the worst; but the latter assume the right of a papal inquisition to arraign before the public the men and the measures of the people, and exclusively and definitively to pass sentence upon them. They even go so far in their publications in the *Chronicle* and in their private discussions and votes as to style themselves the people and to criminate the President and other servants of the public as if they had been created to office by the voice of their clubs alone.[54]

Much as armed resistance to the laws in western Pennsylvania had been crushed by overwhelming public disapproval, the popular societies could not survive in the aftermath of the rebellion and Washington's condemnation. By the end of 1795, they had completely disappeared.

Yet destruction of the democratic clubs could hardly staunch the swelling tide of popular involvement. Neither could the more ferocious effort to suppress the opposition press in 1798, although the latter did drive Jefferson and Madison to new extremes. By almost any measure—voter turnout, men involved in popular electioneering in localities around the country, popular festivities and protest meetings, or the number of newspapers in the country—thousands mobilized as they had never done before. And if they mobilized increasingly to press their own ideas and interests, if they mobilized, not least, to protest gentry disrespect, that is precisely what some gentlemen had hoped that they would do—and just what others, out of self-defense and the necessities of representative democracy, had inadvertently encouraged and promoted. John Adams's "Davila" did produce a national debate on aristocracy and balanced constitutions, although the consequences hounded him to his defeat in 1800.[55] Alexander Hamilton's attack on Jefferson's connection with Freneau not only pitted him against a greater revolutionary hero in a contest that did much to transform Jefferson into the living symbol of democracy but also forced the opposition to develop the ideas that gradually transformed a governmental faction into something like a national party. Indeed, no major national figure of the 1790s wrote as many popular defenses and attacks as Hamilton himself. It thus seems wholly fitting that the decade ended with a pamphlet in which Hamilton accomplished the destruction of his own capacity for future national leadership as well as the destruction of John Adams.[56] Jefferson and Madison went on, of course, to master the techniques of gentry leadership of a republic.

NOTES

1. Speeches of William Grayson, Patrick Henry, and George Mason at the Virginia Ratifying Convention, *Documentary History of the Ratification of the Constitution* (hereafter *DHRC*) (Madison: State Historical Society of Wisconsin, 1976–), 9:1170, 936–37, 1068, 937–38. See also the earlier discussion, pp. 42–43, of "Brutus" and "The Federal Farmer."

2. Gordon S. Wood, *The Creation of the American Republic, 1776–1787* (Chapel Hill: University of North Carolina Press, 1969), 513–14.

3. See, further, Wood's *The Radicalism of the American Revolution* (New York: Knopf, 1991), and compare Stanley Elkins and Eric McKitrick, *The Age of Federalism: The Early American Republic, 1788–1800* (New York: Oxford University Press, 1993), 703, where Madison is particularly identified with this view (as he often is by Wood): Gentlemen of "birth, breeding, refinement, and independent circumstances" understood themselves as "endowed with a special wideness of vision and . . . thus peculiarly fitted to dedicate talent and wisdom to disinterested public service" but as besieged by "the advancing forces of insolence, vulgarity, disorder, self-interest, faction, and demagoguery."

4. *Federalist* 45, 311–14.

5. The Constitution did, however, forbid the states to pass the specific sorts of legislation—tender laws, alterations of private contracts, and other infringements on property rights—that had most alarmed its framers.

6. See p. 41. But consider, as well, that this is not to say that even Hamilton desired a government not grounded firmly on consent. Indeed, at Philadelphia, he strongly favored an enlargement of the House of Representatives to make it more responsive to the people.

7. See Hamilton's speech of June 18, in *Records of the Federal Constitution of 1787* (hereafter *RFC*), ed. Max Farrand, 4 vols. (New Haven, Conn.: Yale University Press, 1937), 1:282–311, and, for his later insistence that he was emotionally committed to a republican system, *RFC*, 1:424, and *The Papers of Alexander Hamilton* (hereafter *PAH*), ed. Harold C. Syrett and Jacob E. Cooke, 26 vols. (New York: Columbia University Press, 1961–1979), 11:443.

8. *Federalist* 51, 351.

9. Actually, in order to allow for the judiciary, Madison did use this definition in *Federalist* 39, 251, but had made it clear in other numbers that it was not sufficient.

10. *Federalist* 39, 250.

11. *Federalist* 10, 62.

12. *Federalist* 46, 318–19; 51, 353; and especially 57, 384–87. But consider, more simply, that the prospect of better representation is clearly identified in *Federalist* 10 itself as a secondary argument for large republics. The major argument is that the great variety among the people will impede formation of factious majorities, and this major argument collapses if the multiplicity of interests among the people is not reflected among the legislators. Laws infringing private rights are made by legislators, not directly by the people.

13. *Federalist* 10, 62–63.

14. *Federalist* 10, 63.

15. *DHRC*, 9:996. If this were not the case, he had admitted, opponents would have been on better ground in their insistence that the Union was too large to be administered as a republic (*Federalist* 14, reading p. 86 in the context developed earlier in the essay).

16. *Federalist* 58, 396. And after these criteria were met, he added, every increase in its size would make it easier for eloquent, ambitious men to dominate its actions; "the countenance of the government may become more democratic, but the soul that animates it will be more oligarchic."

17. *Federalist* 57, 384–87.

18. *Federalist* 57, 386.

19. *Federalist* 58, 396. And see, more broadly, *Federalist* numbers 48–50.

20. "Vices of the Political System of the U.S.," *The Papers of James Madison* (hereafter *PJM*), ed. William T. Hutchinson et al. (Chicago: University Press, 1962–), 9:345–57; *Federalist* 10, 62.

21. James Madison to Thomas Jefferson, October 24, 1787, *PJM*, 10:214.

22. Jean Yarbrough, "Republicanism Reconsidered: Some Thoughts on the Foundation and Preservation of the American Republic," *Review of Politics* 41 (1979): 61–95.

23. *Federalist* 10, 60.

24. David Waldstreicher, *In the Midst of Perpetual Fetes: The Making of American Nationalism, 1776–1820* (Chapel Hill: University of North Carolina Press, 1997), and Simon P. Newman, *Parades and the Politics of the Streets: Festive Culture in the Early American Republic* (Philadelphia: University of Pennsylvania Press, 1997), discuss the revolutionary origins of rising popular involvement and describe its acceleration during the 1790s.

25. Speech of April 28, 1789, *PJM*, 12:119; Lance Banning, *The Sacred Fire of Liberty: James Madison and the Founding of the Federal Republic* (Ithaca, N.Y.: Cornell University Press, 1995), 301–2.

26. On March 30, 1792, Benjamin Rush, the Philadelphia physician, recorded a conversation at Madison's boardinghouse about the "evils introduced into our country by the funded debt." Madison said "that he could at all times discover a sympathy between the speeches and the pockets of all those members of Congress who held certificates" (*PJM*, 14:272, n. 1). And on June 12, Madison sent Jefferson a list that the latter had requested (now lost) so that he could name to the president congressmen corrupted in this way (*PJM*, 14:314–15, 318). By this time, Madison, as well as Jefferson, was telling Washington that the Federalists "were in general unfriendly to republican government and probably aimed at a gradual approximation of ours to a mixed monarchy" (*PJM*, 14:299–304).

27. For exceptions, some of them anticipating the Virginians' full-blown critique of the Federalist system, see Lance Banning, *The Jeffersonian Persuasion: Evolution of a Party Ideology* (Ithaca, N.Y.: Cornell University Press, 1978), 149–52. On balance, nonetheless, the population and the press were less critical of Congress during its third session than they had been in 1789 and 1790, and virtually all studies, including Waldstreicher and Newman, date the great explosion of popular politics to the years

after 1793, when the French Revolution and the European wars introduced additional issues.

28. See, especially, Jefferson to George Mason, February 4, 1791, written two days after Madison's speech against the bank (*The Papers of Thomas Jefferson* [hereafter *PTJ*], ed. Julian P. Boyd et al. [Princeton, N.J.: Princeton University Press, 1950–], 19:241–42): The firm establishment of the new, revolutionary government in France, Jefferson wrote, might be necessary "to stay up our own and to prevent it from falling back to that kind of halfway house, the English constitution. It cannot be denied that we have among us a sect who believe [the English constitution] to contain whatever is perfect in human institutions; that the members of this sect have, many of them, names and offices which stand high in the estimation of our countrymen. . . . The only corrective of what is amiss in our present government will be the augmentation of the numbers in the lower house, so as to get a more agricultural representation, which may put that interest above that of the stockjobbers." See also Jefferson to James Innes, March 13, 1791 (*PTJ*, 19:543): "It is fortunate that our first executive magistrate is purely and jealously republican. We cannot expect all his successors to be so, and therefore should avail ourselves of the present day to establish principles and examples which may fence us against future heresies preached now, to be practised hereafter."

29. Jefferson to Thomas Mann Randolph Jr., May 15, 1791, *PTJ*, 20:416.

30. Whether Jefferson or Madison initiated the idea for such a paper is impossible to know. Its launching, though, was certainly a product of their close collaboration. Madison had long been looking for a federal position for Freneau, knew that he was planning to start a paper, and persisted in the effort to persuade him to move to Philadelphia rather than rural New Jersey even after Freneau declined Jefferson's initial offer and Jefferson turned instead toward trying to persuade Benjamin Franklin Bache to turn his *General Advertiser* into a national paper. Success in the negotiation was apparently sealed when the two Virginians had breakfast with Freneau in New York on May 20, 1791, just before they departed on a holiday to Lake Champlain and on into New England.

31. Jefferson's correspondence on this matter is published as a set in *PTJ*, 20:290–312, with a helpful editorial note at 268–290.

32. Madison to Jefferson, May 12, 1791, *PJM*, 14:22–23. For a fuller discussion of Adams's writings, including some of the quotations that got him in the most serious trouble, see Banning, *The Sacred Fire of Liberty*, 338–40. C. Bradley Thompson, *John Adams and the Spirit of Liberty* (Lawrence: University Press of Kansas, 1991), is the fullest, most recent study of Adams's thought, but it is not completely satisfying on the reasons why so many bitterly objected.

33. These are reprinted in Worthington Chauncy Ford, ed., *The Writings of John Quincy Adams* (New York: Macmillan, 1913), 1:65–110.

34. Banning, *The Jeffersonian Persuasion*, 156–59.

35. The essays on consolidation and a sound interpretation of the Constitution are discussed on p. 47.

36. "Government of the United States," *National Gazette*, February 4, 1792, reprinted in *PJM*, 14:218.

37. "Public Opinion," *National Gazette*, December 19, 1791, *PJM*, 14:178. For a recent article emphasizing Madison's preoccupation with public opinion in his essays of the early 1790s and for the likely influence on Madison of recent French writers on the subject, see Colleen A. Sheehan, "Madison and the French Enlightenment: The Authority of Public Opinion," *William and Mary Quarterly* 59 (2002): 925–56.

38. This blends "Public Opinion" with "Consolidation," *National Gazette*, December 3, 1791, *PJM*, 14:137–39.

39. "Public Opinion," *PJM* 14:178. Waldstreicher is particularly instructive for his insistence that newspaper accounts of parades, feasts, toasts, and other popular actions were integral aspects of the "politics of the streets."

40. "Who Are the Best Keepers of the People's Liberties?" *National Gazette*, December 20, 1792, *PJM*, 14:426–27.

41. Hamilton's attack on Jefferson, opening with the letter signed "T.L." in the *Gazette of the United States* for July 25, 1792, and continuing under an array of different pseudonyms, can be followed in full in *PAH*, vols. 12 and 13.

42. See Philip M. Marsh, *Monroe's Defense of Jefferson and Freneau against Hamilton* (Oxford, Ohio: n.p., 1948), and Banning, *The Jeffersonian Persuasion*, 172–76.

43. Madison to Jefferson, September 2, 1793, *PJM*, 15:92–93. See also Madison to Jefferson, September 1, 1793, *PJM*, 15:87–88, which enclosed a copy of model resolutions for Archibald Stuart, whom Madison hoped would introduce them to a meeting in Staunton. The best antidote to the petitions from the towns would be "a true and authentic expression of the sense of the people," which would have to be collected by "temperate and respectable men who have the opportunity of meeting them." "The voice of particular places . . . may otherwise be mistaken for that of the nation."

44. The resolutions are printed with a useful editorial note in *PJM*, 15:76–80. They were the first of several such efforts Madison would organize during the 1790s.

45. Thirty-five or forty of these popular societies emerged throughout the country in the aftermath of proclamation of the French Republic. Eugene Perry Link, *Democratic-Republican Societies, 1790–1800* (New York: Columbia University Press, 1942), remains the standard study. See also Philip S. Foner, *The Democratic-Republican Societies, 1790–1800: A Documentary Sourcebook of Constitutions, Declarations, Addresses, Resolutions, and Toasts* (Westport,

Conn.: Greenwood, 1976), and Matthew Schoenbachler, "Republicanism in the Age of Democratic Revolution: The Democratic-Republican Societies of the 1790s," *Journal of the Early Republic* 18 (summer 1998): 237–61.

46. Adams's insistence that aristocrats could be controlled only by isolating them in one of two legislative houses was grounded, in part, on his conviction that the people would always find it easier to prefer wealth, birth, beauty, and the like to genuine merit. The famous, late-life discussions of natural aristocracy between Adams and Jefferson, available in Lester J. Cappon, ed., *The Adams-Jefferson Letters*, 2 vols. (New York: Simon & Schuster, 1971), especially 2:371–72, are instructive on this point.

47. Officers and members of the Mingo Creek, Yough, and Washington County societies *were* heavily involved in the insurrection, but other clubs throughout the country, not to mention Republican politicians, strongly condemned armed resistance to the law; and it has been well said that the Philadelphia society "could have made a quorum" in the army that marched against it. See John C. Miller, *The Federalist Era, 1789–1801* (New York: Harper & Row, 1960), 161.

48. Madison to James Monroe, December 4, 1794, *PJM* 15:406.

49. Madison to James Monroe, December 4, 1794, *PJM*, 15:406. Writing to Jefferson on November 30, Madison went even further, calling it an "attack on the most sacred principles of our Constitution" (*PJM*, 15:396). Characteristically, however, both Madison and Jefferson tried to see Washington as the unwitting dupe of Hamilton and other plotters. "The game," wrote Madison, "was to connect the democratic societies with the odium of the insurrection—to connect the Republicans in Congress with those societies—[and] to put the President ostensibly at the head of the other party, in opposition to both" (*PJM*, 15:406).

50. Speech of November 27, 1794, *PJM*, 15:391.

51. Madison to James Monroe, April 12, 1794, *PJM*, 15:407.

52. Elkins and McKitrick, *The Age of Federalism*, 455–61, 482–83, is brilliant on this point and on the quick collapse and easy defeat of the Whiskey Rebellion by the concept of popular sovereignty.

53. February 1794. Quoted in Elkins and McKitrick, *The Age of Federalism*, 460, from Foner, *The Democratic-Republican Societies, 1790–1800*, 154.

54. "For the [Boston] *Columbian Centinel*," September 27, 1794. The *Independent Chronicle* was the leading Republican newspaper in Boston. The Society of the Cincinnati, founded by Continental officers at the end of the Revolutionary War, had provoked a major controversy by providing that membership would be hereditary.

55. Adams's belligerent replies to the flood of patriotic addresses from militia companies and other groups during the quasi-war with France were yet another, usually neglected, landmark in the rise of popular involvement.

56. His "Letter from Alexander Hamilton concerning the Public Conduct and Character of John Adams, Esq., President of the United States," a critical incident in the wreck of Federalist unity in the campaign of 1800, came within a hair of calling Adams insane. It was perceived as so intemperate and ill-advised that it blasted Hamilton's reputation as badly as Adams's. The best discussion of its effects on both men's reputation is Joanne B. Freeman, *Affairs of Honor: National Politics in the Early Republic* (New Haven, Conn.: Yale University Press, 2001), chap. 3.

Index

About the Author

Lance Banning is professor of history at the University of Kentucky, where he has taught since 1973. A native of Kansas City, he received his B.A. from the University of Missouri at Kansas City in 1964 and his M.A. and Ph.D. degrees from Washington University (St. Louis) in 1968 and 1971. He has held fellowships from the National Endowment for the Humanities, the John Simon Guggenheim Foundation, the National Humanities Center, and the Center for the History of Freedom. Banning is coeditor of the University Press of Kansas series American Political Thought, editor of *After the Constitution: Party Conflict in the New Republic* (Belmont, Calif.: Wadsworth, 1989), and author of many articles and essays on the American founding and the first party struggle. His first book, *The Jeffersonian Persuasion: Evolution of a Party Ideology* (Ithaca, N.Y.: Cornell University Press, 1978), received the international book award of Phi Alpha Theta and was nominated by the press for Pulitzer, Bancroft, and other prizes. *Jefferson and Madison: Three Conversations from the Founding*, a revision of his 1992 Merrill Jensen Lectures at the University of Wisconsin, and *The Sacred Fire of Liberty: James Madison and the Founding of the Federal Republic* were published in 1995. The latter received the Merle Curti Award in Intellectual History from the Organization of American Historians and was a finalist for the Pulitzer Prize. During the spring of 1997, Banning held the John Adams Chair in American History, a senior Fulbright appointment, at the University of Groningen in the Netherlands. During the fall of 2001, he was Leverhulme Visiting Professor at the University of Edinburgh.